THE UNIVERSAL DECLARATION OF
HUMAN RIGHTS IN THE 21st CENTURY

The Universal Declaration of Human Rights in the 21st Century:

A Living Document in a Changing World

A report by the
Global Citizenship Commission

Edited by Gordon Brown

GLOBAL INSTITUTE FOR
ADVANCED STUDY

NYU

OpenBook
Publishers

https://www.openbookpublishers.com

The views and opinions expressed in this report do not necessarily reflect the views, opinions, or official policy of any organization with which any individual Commissioner may be affiliated, or of members of those organizations.

ISBN Paperback: 978-1-78374-218-9
ISBN Hardback: 978-1-78374-219-6
ISBN Digital (PDF): 978-1-78374-220-2
ISBN Digital ebook (epub): 978-1-78374-221-9
ISBN Digital ebook (mobi): 978-1-78374-222-6
DOI: 10.11647/OBP.0091

Cover image: "In Our Hands" (2010) by Charamelody, CC BY-NC 2.0, https://www.flickr.com/photos/charamelody/4546946888

All paper used by Open Book Publishers is SFI (Sustainable Forestry Initiative), PEFC (Programme for the Endorsement of Forest Certification Schemes) and Forest Stewardship Council(r)(FSC(r) certified.

Printed in the United Kingdom, United States and Australia
by Lightning Source for Open Book Publishers (Cambridge, UK).

Contents

Glossary

CAT	Convention Against Torture and Other Cruel, Inhuman or Degrading Treatment or Punishment
CEDAW	The Convention on the Elimination of all Forms of Discrimination Against Women
CRC	Convention on the Rights of the Child
CRPD	Convention on the Rights of Persons with Disabilities
CSOs	Civil Society Organizations
GCC	Global Citizenship Commission
EFA	Education for All
GIAS	Global Institute for Advanced Study
HRE	Human Rights Education
ICCPR	International Covenant on Civil and Political Rights
ICERD	International Convention on the Elimination of All Forms of Racial Discrimination
ICESCR	International Covenant on Economic, Social and Cultural Rights
ILO	International Labour Organization
MDGs	Millennium Development Goals
OHCHR	Office of the High Commission for Human Rights
OPCAT	Optional Protocol to CAT

The P5	Permanent Members of the Security Council
RtoP	Responsibility to Protect
SDGs	Sustainable Development Goals
UNESCO	United Nations Educational, Scientific and Cultural Organization
UNHCR	United Nations High Commissioner for Refugees
UPR	Universal Periodic Review

Introduction

by Gordon Brown

When the Universal Declaration of Human Rights (**UDHR**) was adopted in 1948,[1] the world was a very different place. Years of war had left the better part of two continents in disarray. A geopolitical reordering saw an Iron Curtain fall across a continent and a Cold War rise across the globe. And the world was waking up to the unconscionable horrors of the Holocaust. From the ruins of the Second World War came a call to enshrine fundamental human rights.

Facilitating this moment of global introspection was a Philosophers' Committee under the direction of the United Nations Educational, Scientific and Cultural Organization (**UNESCO**). The Committee enlisted leading thinkers – from Mahatma Gandhi to Aldous Huxley – to contribute their insights about a proposed Universal Declaration of Human Rights. The work of the Philosophers' Committee was then passed to the UN Human Rights Commission, chaired by Eleanor Roosevelt, a tireless fighter whose supreme and lasting achievement was shaping a human rights consensus among the then 58 UN Member States.

The framers of the Declaration envisaged three parts to the postwar human rights enterprise: a set of general principles, the codification of those principles into law, and a practical means of implementation. Because of the divisions and hostilities of the Cold War, countries could neither agree on the basis of human rights, nor on how specific rights should be upheld. So it was that Eleanor Roosevelt could only complete

---

1   An annotated version of the Universal Declaration of Human Rights is set out in Appendix A.

    http://dx.doi.org/10.11647/OBP.0091.01

the first task. But owing in large part to her vision and leadership, the nations of the world did issue a historic declaration of human rights – a pantheon that for the first time encompassed civil, political, social, and economic rights. It is a Universal Declaration that has withstood the test of time.

As the Declaration's seventieth anniversary nears, we are reminded that its age has hastened an evolution, bequeathing to us something both inspirational and demanding. Today, the UDHR provides a "common conscience" for humanity. It is a beacon of hope. It is also a call for action, setting a high standard by which we judge the width of our generosity, the depth of our compassion, and the breadth of our humanity. It sends forth a message that injustice anywhere is a threat to justice everywhere, and that no evil can last forever.

And everywhere we look we are reminded that the Declaration has stirred civil rights movements and hastened the march of progress. The words of protestors speaking out against colonialism and apartheid have been laced with the spirit, and at times the letter, of the Declaration. Those seeking to discriminate on the basis of ethnicity, religion, gender, and sexual orientation have confronted a wall – and a tall one at that – in the Declaration. Conditions of poverty, illiteracy, and squalor have all been challenged under the banner of the Declaration. And for those like Nelson Mandela, inspired by the sentiments of the Declaration, no intimidation, no show trial, no prison cell – not even the threat of execution – could ever extinguish their desire to stand for freedom.

This is not to turn a blind eye to injustices that endure; for every step we take there are two that have yet to be made. Nonetheless, the Declaration is a proven force for good – both weapon and symbol for those seeking to give strength to the weak, courage to the fainthearted, power to the powerless, and voice to the silent. The very existence of a universal declaration rebukes long-standing, but intellectually feeble presumptions, that a sovereign state's treatment of its citizens is the business of that state and that state alone. Time and again the arc of recent history has been altered by the Universal Declaration of Human Rights.

The Global Citizenship Commission (*GCC*), designed to reflect on that progress and the demands of the future, was born in the classroom. With the guidance of John Sexton, President of New York University

(*NYU*) from 2002 to 2015, the Commission's members met in a series of seminars to discuss the UDHR's continuing relevance and contribution to the development of a global ethic.[2] We understood we were asking questions about a new world – a sphere far more interconnected, integrated, and interdependent than when the Declaration was signed. More than ever before, the lives of each of us are affected by the lives of all of us. This is the lens through which realities were viewed and questions shaped. Principally, we focused on how the Declaration is understood for those born after 1948, and thus into a world where these rights are known. In parallel, discussions with UN Secretary-General Ban Ki-moon stressed the centrality of individual citizens' rights and the need for a strong educational foundation. This dual emphasis, reflected throughout our report, accords with Eleanor Roosevelt's statement that ideals "carry no weight unless the people know them, unless the people understand them, unless the people demand that they be lived."

Drawing on the Declaration's own history, the Commission borrowed a page from the UDHR and convened a Philosophers' Committee.[3] Its work informed the deliberations of a global working group of scholars, led by the highly-respected Professor Jeremy Waldron. The Philosophers' Committee's analysis provided the academic foundation for a meaningful examination of the UDHR, and I join the Commission in thanking these scholars for their pioneering work.

In light of the Philosophers' Committee's analysis, the Commission's report first considers how our understanding of human rights has evolved. We then move on to identify specific rights requiring more emphasis than they received in the Declaration, if they were acknowledged at all. As one might expect, the rights of women, children, the disabled, and the LGBT community require further attention and a deepened global commitment. What is more, in a world where 60 million individuals are displaced from their homes and 20 million are refugees, the rights of migrants and stateless persons have become once again – as was true in the upheavals following the Second World War – a matter of vital importance. The report also examines what justification there can ever be for derogations of rights, how we combine civil and political

---

2   The members of the Commission are set out in Appendix B.
3   The members of the Philosophers' Committee are set out in Appendix C.

rights with social and economic rights, and who must ultimately take responsibility for upholding the UDHR as a global ethic – as a covenant.

These questions were flanked by a recognition of reality – the hard data proving there is much work to be done. Discussions with the Secretary-General, the UN High Commissioner for Human Rights Zeid Ra'ad Al Hussein, and my own experiences as UN Special Envoy for Global Education convinced me that a balanced Commission report should address failures of implementation. This is, in a real sense, the unfinished work of Eleanor Roosevelt's commission. Even after almost seventy years, the question of how we protect enshrined rights has never been answered comprehensively.

The Commission's report is a reminder of what is at stake. Accordingly, we advance recommendations that highlight the urgent need to strengthen human rights in the twenty-first century. Some recommendations call for upholding specific rights in new ways, such as our proposal urging the international community to adopt a more far-reaching convention on refugees and migrants and our call for an International Children's Court. Other recommendations call attention to deeper, structural issues, including our conclusion that countries may not hide behind the thin veil of national sovereignty as a pretext for insulating themselves from external human rights pressures. We advocate enhancing the UN's system for upholding and advancing human rights with a proposal that Security Council members voluntarily suspend veto rights in situations involving mass atrocities.

I am honored to have chaired the Global Citizenship Commission. I am profoundly grateful to each Commissioner for making this report, and its proposals, possible. Over two years, the Commission met in Edinburgh, Bonn, Abu Dhabi, Dubai, and New York – all while holding global consultations drawing on counsel and expertise from China, Latin America, and Sub-Saharan Africa. During the life of the Commission, we endeavored – through public dialogues and external consultation – to include a broad range of perspectives. All of this has been made possible by the generous support of New York University, the Carnegie UK Trust, the University of Edinburgh, the University of Bonn, and the NYU Global Institute for Advanced Study (*GIAS*), chaired by Paul Boghossian who has been an ever-present influence for good. We are grateful to the Director of Research and Secretary to the

Commission, Andrew Hilland, and our Staff Directors Melissa Friesen and Michael Patullo, all of whom carried the burden of servicing our work for two years. And we owe a special debt of gratitude to Executive Director Diane Yu who managed this process, and Robert Shrum for his guidance in drafting the Commission's report. I want to thank all those who helped make this report possible, including the individuals and institutions mentioned in the Acknowledgments.

Voices at the margins must come alive. For this reason, I believe this report can make a valuable contribution to contemporary debates. We write of course from a comfortable vantage point – from a promontory. Wherever we direct our gaze, we are bound to find broken refugees, oppressed children, and enslaved women. We see them and, in turn, hope they see us and demand action. I do not expect our report to be, like the Declaration itself, timeless. But I do hope it will be timely, holding high once again the challenge posed to each successive generation – to do better and achieve more. The Commission is insistent that rights imply responsibilities. In securing certain rights, and seeking to enshrine others, we are constantly reminded of both how far the world has come and how much farther we must go. For we must never forget that the global condition of human rights – civil, political, social, and economic – is the yardstick with which we measure humanity's progress.

Gordon Brown
Former Prime Minister of the United Kingdom
UN Special Envoy for Global Education

Preface
by Paul Boghossian

This report by the Global Citizenship Commission is the first of the Global Institute for Advanced Study's major initiatives to be brought to fruition. It gives me great pride that the Institute's inaugural achievement is represented by such an important document.

The GIAS is a nascent initiative at New York University that helps support innovative and (typically) interdisciplinary scholarly work requiring collaboration on an international scale and with a sustained, multi-year focus. Conceived in conversations between (then) Vice-Chancellor Richard Foley and me, and with the crucial support of President John Sexton and Provost David McLaughlin, it was launched in 2011. All three of these leaders of NYU deserve thanks for their willingness to invest significant resources in encouraging unusual, risky, but potentially transformative work.

When Gordon Brown approached me in 2012 with his idea to convene a commission that would study the continuing relevance to our time of the Universal Declaration of Human Rights, and its contribution to the development of a global ethic, it struck me both as an enormously important idea and as a perfect fit for the mission of the Global Institute.

After some discussion, Gordon and I agreed that it would be best if the project were to proceed in two phases. In the first, a distinguished committee of academics – philosophers, political theorists, and human rights lawyers – would lay the intellectual groundwork for the commission's report by providing a detailed analytical commentary on the UDHR. In the second phase, a blue ribbon commission, chaired by Gordon, would use the findings of this "Philosophers' Committee" to

© NYU GIAS, CC BY   http://dx.doi.org/10.11647/OBP.0091.02

develop a report that would be presented, at his request, to Ban Ki-moon, the Secretary-General of the United Nations, and distributed widely.

The road to the successful completion of this report has been a long one, involving three meetings of the Philosophers' Committee, six meetings of the Global Citizenship Commission, and countless meetings of the Commission's Steering Committee, which I chaired. I am grateful to Professors Michael Forster and Markus Gabriel for hosting our meetings in Bonn, Germany. I want especially to thank the members of the Steering Committee, Anthony Appiah, Emma Rothschild, Robert Shrum, Jeremy Waldron, and Diane Yu, for their hard work between meetings of the full Commission that made progress at those meetings possible. Andrew Hilland and Melissa Friesen provided indispensable support.

I am very grateful to Professor Jeremy Waldron of NYU's Law School for accepting our invitation to lead the Philosophers' Committee. Jeremy assembled a superb panel of scholars, and worked tirelessly in all its different phases to bring this report into existence.

I am also immensely grateful to Gordon Brown for entrusting this important project to the GIAS, for his unflagging enthusiasm and energy for it, and, in general, for his unwavering dedication to making the world a better place.

Paul Boghossian,
Director, GIAS
Julius Silver Professor of Philosophy
NYU

Acknowledgments

The Global Institute for Advanced Study at New York University and the NYU Office of the President were pleased to provide academic, financial, and administrative support for the work of the Global Citizenship Commission, from the first meeting of the Philosophers' Committee in the fall of 2012 to the present day. The vision of Gordon Brown in undertaking this vital work for submission to UN Secretary-General Ban Ki-moon has inspired all of us, and we hope that *The Universal Declaration of Human Rights in the 21st Century* will make a profound and lasting impact.

As Executive Director of the Commission, I wish to acknowledge a number of individuals and institutions that helped make this report possible. I am grateful to the members of the Philosophers' Committee – and its Chair, Jeremy Waldron – whose brilliant analysis provided the academic underpinning of the report. I want to thank the GCC Steering Committee, in which I had the pleasure of participating alongside the Committee Chair, Paul Boghossian, and members Anthony Appiah, Emma Rothschild, Robert Shrum, and Jeremy Waldron. Melissa Friesen (2014–2016) and Michael Patullo (2013–2014) served as Staff Directors to the Commission, providing outstanding administrative and logistical support to Commission Chair Gordon Brown and the Commissioners. Andrew Hilland, Director of Research and Secretary to the Commission, was invaluable in helping to produce the final version of the report. In addition, this report would not have been possible without the support of John Sexton and Andrew Hamilton, the immediate past and current Presidents of NYU, respectively.

          http://dx.doi.org/10.11647/OBP.0091.03

I am grateful for the assistance and support of the following people in hosting meetings and public-facing events of the GCC: Timothy O'Shea (Principal, University of Edinburgh), Charlie Jeffery (Vice Principal for Public Policy and Impact, University of Edinburgh), and Martyn Evans (Chief Executive, Carnegie Trust UK) for the Commission's meeting in Edinburgh in October 2013; Jürgen Fohrmann (former Rector, University of Bonn), Michael Forster (Alexander von Humboldt Professor, Chair for Theoretical Philosophy, and Co-Director of the International Center for Philosophy, University of Bonn), Markus Gabriel (Chair for Epistemology and Co-Director of the International Center for Philosophy, University of Bonn), Dieter Sturma (Chair for Philosophy of Ethics and the Biosciences and Director of the Institute for Science and Politics, University of Bonn), and Stefan Zimmermann (International Center for Philosophy, University of Bonn) for the Commission's meeting in Bonn in May 2014; and Klaus Schwab (Founder and Executive Chairman, World Economic Forum), Alfred Bloom (Vice Chancellor, NYU Abu Dhabi), Fabio Piano (Provost, NYU Abu Dhabi), Reindert Falkenburg, Gila Bessarat Waels, Antoine El Khayat, Nora Yousef, Nils Lewis, and Danielle Cherubin (of the NYU Abu Dhabi Institute) for the Commission's meetings in Abu Dhabi and Dubai in November 2014. The assistance of NYU administrators John Beckman, Regina Drew, and Gregory Albanis from the Office of University Relations and Public Affairs in mounting the public forum in New York in April 2016 was also much appreciated.

I want to thank the Center on Global Justice (University of California, San Diego), of which Commissioner Fonna Forman is Founding Co-Director, for undertaking comprehensive research and analysis on human rights implementation and human rights education. In particular, I am grateful to the implementation research team, which was supervised by Sean Morgan and also included John Gotti, Vanessa Lodermeier, Mike Nicholson, and John Porten. I am also grateful to Monisha Bajaj, Ben Cislaghi, and Gerry Mackie, who authored the Online Appendix D to this report,[1] *Advancing Transformative Human Rights Education*, and to Commissioner Andrew Forrest and the Minderoo Foundation for providing material support for their work.

---

1   Online Appendix D, on Human Rights Education, is available at https://www. openbookpublishers.com/isbn/9781783742189#resources

We have benefitted immensely from the input and advice of UN High Commissioner for Human Rights Zeid Ra'ad Al Hussein, and an array of lawyers from his office, including Gianni Magazzeni (Chief of the Americas, Europe and Central Asia Branch, Field Operations and Technical Cooperation Division) and Mona Rishmawi (Rule of Law and Democracy Section). Zainab Hawa Bangura, United Nations Under-Secretary-General and Special Representative of the Secretary-General on Sexual Violence in Conflict, participated in the deliberations of the Commission. Aung San Suu Kyi was a member of the Commission but due to events in Myanmar was unable to contribute to our final deliberations. Finally, we have been fortunate to be able to draw on the expertise of Philip Alston (NYU Law School), Itai Madamombe (Assistant to the UN Secretary-General), Dimitrina Petrova (Founding Executive Director, Equal Rights Trust), Michael Posner (Co-Director, NYU Stern's Center for Business and Human Rights), and Michael Sandel (Harvard University, Department of Government).

Diane C. Yu
GCC Executive Director
Counselor to Leadership and Executive Director
Sheikh Mohamed bin Zayed Community Programs at NYU Abu Dhabi

Executive Summary

The Long and Influential Life of the Universal Declaration of Human Rights

The Universal Declaration of Human Rights is a monumental embodiment for our time of the ancient idea that we all belong to a single global community, and that each human being has moral ties and responsibilities to all others.

From the start, endorsed and adopted in 1948 by most Member States of the UN, the Declaration has been a beacon and a standard, its influence both wide and deep. The UDHR has been and is an unprecedented educational and cultural force, making people conversant with the idea of human rights, providing a widely accepted text enumerating those rights, delivering an articulate focus for what might otherwise be timid and inarticulate concerns, and sending out a message that an injustice anywhere is a threat to justice everywhere. Today, the UDHR, translated into 350 languages, is the best-known and most often cited human rights document on Earth. By setting out, for the first time, fundamental rights to be universally protected, it is a milestone in the history of human interactions and the cause of human rights.

The Global Citizenship Commission both affirms the continuing relevance and inspirational force of the UDHR and seeks further recognition and respect for human rights for all citizens of the world, in light of developments in the twenty-first century. The social, political, and legal environment has been transformed since 1948, and our global

http://dx.doi.org/10.11647/OBP.0091.04

interconnectedness and dependence have diminished our moral distance. Yet as a living document, the UDHR demands renewed attention and speaks urgently to the issues of today. In this report, we assess the life to date of the UDHR: its foundational principles, its profound impact, and its legacy. We consider the evolving understanding of human rights and identify certain rights that were not addressed specifically in the 1948 document but that arguably reflect our understanding of rights today. We examine the issues of limitations and derogations, social and economic rights, where the responsibility for upholding human rights lies, and – critically – implementation.

The cornerstone of the Declaration is the concept of human dignity: "recognition of the inherent dignity and of the equal and inalienable rights of all members of the human family is the foundation of freedom, justice and peace in the world." Sadly, for millions of people, the recognition of their inherent dignity is far from a reality. To us, this speaks not of the failure of the UDHR but of the need to keep re-examining the relevance of these standards, and to continue to challenge ourselves to find better ways to achieve our shared goal of a common human dignity.

The Evolving Understanding of Rights

Globalization has changed the terms of interaction in global life, and it has created space both for implicit extensions of and explicit additions to the content of human rights doctrine. Since 1948 there have been many important human rights conventions that have addressed some of the issues we identify. Nevertheless, it is essential to recognize a number of rights that we think have come into clearer focus after seventy years and need more emphasis than they received in the Declaration. These fall into three broad categories.

First, the *rights of members of specific groups*, comprising the rights of women; the rights of children; the rights of the disabled, including the profoundly disabled; rights related to sexual orientation; and the rights of prisoners.

Second, the *rights of groups as such*, comprising the right to national self-determination, including regional autonomy and subsidiarity; the rights of indigenous peoples; the prohibition against ethnic cleansing;

and the rights of peoples prejudiced at the national or communal level by climate change.

Third, *rights related to other issues affecting vital interests*, comprising migration; statelessness; administrative justice; corruption; privacy from state or corporate electronic surveillance; access to the Internet and electronic communication on a global scale; extreme poverty and deep inequality; healthcare; and a safe, clean, healthy, and sustainable environment.

Each of these issues demands the international community's attention, some because of the need for a clear articulation and recognition of rights and all because of the need to take concrete steps to ensure their implementation. For example, on the issue of migration, the Commission recommends that the international community urgently:

> Implement Sustainable Development Goal (**SDG**) 10.7, which calls for states to "facilitate orderly, safe, regular and responsible migration and mobility of people, including through the implementation of planned and well-managed migration policies."

> Strengthen the international refugee protection system.

> Consider adopting a new international convention on refugees and migrants.

And to ensure the protection of the rights of children, we recommend that:

> The international community support the creation of a Children's Court, with the power to receive and adjudicate petitions from children and their representatives on violations of the Convention on the Rights of the Child, to issue legally binding judgments, and to investigate areas of concern such as child labor, child slavery, and child marriage.

> The International Criminal Court investigates and prosecutes crimes against children within its remit to the full extent of the law.

The UN Security Council convenes a "Children's Council" – an annual review on children's rights, building on its existing debate of the plight of children in armed conflict.

At the national level, all states create accessible complaint mechanisms for the resolution of violations of the rights of children, and consider establishing a Youth Parliament, Children's Commissioner, and dedicated budget for Children.

Limitations and Derogations

Article 29(2) of the UDHR sets out the circumstances in which limitations on individual rights are permissible. The Declaration as a whole should be read as the assertion of a strong presumption in favor of human rights and Article 29(2) should be read as placing the burden of proof on anyone who seeks to limit them.

Unlike the UDHR, the International Covenant on Civil and Political Rights (**ICCPR**) makes separate and extensive provision for the derogation of rights in national and/or international emergencies. However, the increasing reliance in the modern world on long-term, continuous states of emergency as justifications for human rights derogations is not dealt with adequately by the ICCPR's formulations, as they envisage relatively short-term, clearly demarcated emergencies. The international community should develop standards governing long-term derogations of human rights in national or international emergencies, to ensure that this process is not abused.

In recent years, there have been military interventions that contravene the UN Charter's prohibition on the use of force. And states have responded to the rise and persistence of international terrorism by employing tactics of surveillance, detention of suspects, and targeted killing. The Commission emphasizes that each of these developments raises human rights issues, and calls on the international community to develop standards governing the use of force and the response to international terrorism that are derived from current conceptions and enduring foundations of human rights.

Lastly, it is critical to take a comprehensive approach to terrorism that encompasses not only essential security-based counter-terrorism measures, but also systematic preventative measures that address the root causes of violent extremism. These include lack of socioeconomic opportunities; marginalization and discrimination; poor governance; violations of human rights and the rule of law; prolonged and unresolved conflicts; and radicalization in prisons. *The creation of open, equitable, inclusive, and pluralist societies, founded on the full respect of human rights and with economic opportunities for all, represents the most tangible and meaningful alternative to violent extremism and the most promising strategy for undermining its appeal.*

Social and Economic Rights

Social and economic rights are vital. They reflect genuine human needs that every state has an obligation to attend to, within existing resources, in the interest of all those committed to their care. We think it is fitting and valuable that the UDHR enshrined social and economic rights in the same document as civil and political rights, and thus to perceive human rights as a whole in the context of a single declaration.

The social and economic provisions of the UDHR should be interpreted to mean that everyone is entitled to certain minimum standards of health, education, and social security. The concept of dignity – while abstract – provides a yardstick against which to set minimum measures. The extent of available resources in each society is one determinative factor, though the UDHR also imposes constraints on the allocation of such resources as there are. *The Commission believes that the UDHR (and the International Covenant on Economic, Social and Cultural Rights (ICESCR)) should be read as endorsing an ongoing global conversation about what the minimum provision should be and a rule of progress to the effect that the human rights framework calls for steps to improve the position of everyone, including the least advantaged in society.*

States have front-line responsibility for the social and economic well-being of their citizens. Fair economic growth has a critical role to play in this, and the Commission believes it is crucial to see a stronger connection between economic policy and the instruments of human rights. It is evident, however, that the challenges faced by many states cannot be resolved entirely by actions in those states alone. There is an overwhelming moral case for interpreting the social and economic rights provisions of the Declaration as placing obligations on the international community to alleviate world poverty. International aid and transfers, aimed at strengthening the capacity of recipient states to secure the social and economic rights of their citizens, thus have an indispensable role to play. Responsibilities among the international community to uphold social and economic rights are in the Commission's view held not only by states, but also above the level of states by international organizations and below the level of states by corporations and individuals.

It is sometimes said that, although the rights in the Declaration are presented as an interconnected body of principles, complementary and mutually supportive, there are in fact serious conflicts among them. It is sometimes argued, for example, that the rights to freedom of speech or assembly may conflict with the right of people not to live in poverty, that the only way to lift large numbers of people out of poverty may involve authoritarian rule. In certain very specific real-world settings, our ability to fully implement one right may conflict with our ability to fully implement another, at least temporarily. However, any such claim would be very hard to establish and must always be subjected to the most rigorous scrutiny. Furthermore, it is always a serious question whether any particular proposed trade-off is morally justifiable.

Responsibility for Human Rights

The UDHR does not specify who carries the responsibilities corresponding to the rights it enumerates. Yet the role of states remains essential. Given the realities of our world – this was even more the case in 1948 – states must be regarded as the main guarantors of the rights of their own citizens. The laws and national constitutions of states, in most instances, will be the first recourse to address any violations of human rights, and should be regarded as the ordinary mode of implementation. In a globalized world, it is also the duty of each state to concern itself to a certain extent with the human rights of persons outside its borders.

While states have the primary responsibility for ensuring the human rights of their citizens, there are numerous examples of situations where governments no longer control substantial tracts of territory, no longer control the military or have a monopoly on force, lack legitimacy, and are unable or unwilling to provide public services. In these situations, who is responsible for the human rights of the population? This issue needs to be urgently addressed by the international community.

The fact that one entity – like a state – has responsibility for a given right is quite compatible with other entities also having their own obligations. Rights generate waves of responsibility, and those responsibilities may fall on an array of duty-bearers. Though national state responsibility is primary, sub-national governments, international institutions, corporations, and private persons each and all have a common duty to ensure recognition of human rights and accept responsibility to secure them. Rights-bearers themselves also have responsibilities with respect to their own rights and responsibilities as rights-bearers to the rights system as a whole and to society generally.

It would be a mistake to develop a rigid or closed model of responsibility for rights, or to conclude that rights are of no value until responsibilities are actually specified. The advantage of specifying rights first is that this provides a basis for thinking about the duties of the state and other entities. *The Commission has judged that it is both sensible and essential to retain an open and developing sense of where responsibilities lie, since the environment in which rights have to be satisfied is constantly changing.*

Implementation of Human Rights

State of play on representative rights

In our examination of the implementation of select rights in the Declaration – the anti-slavery provision; the anti-torture provision; the free expression provision and the free association provision; and the education provision – a number of themes emerged. First, the UDHR represents the founding document in a process of progressive elaboration of human rights. Second, historic progress has been made in the promotion and protection of rights since 1948, including the development of a body of human rights law and implementation mechanisms that simply could not have been envisioned in the 1920s and 1930s. Third, despite the gains, we must recognize and respond to the reality that human rights continue to be violated on an alarming scale across the globe. Fourth, the fullness of human rights will only be achieved through multiple overlapping and coordinated mechanisms – that operate at both the international and national levels, and which engage both governmental and non-governmental institutions.

Suggestions on implementation

The Commission analyzes and advances recommendations in respect of four areas.

UN system of human rights implementation

The Commission supports a number of existing proposals for improving the UN system for the protection of human rights. We call on the UN to establish a commission to consider these and other proposals for realizing Article 28 of the Declaration.

> The UN should seek to ensure that the problems and priorities identified through UN human rights mechanisms command sufficient attention and action from the international community and the UN as a whole, including its security and development endeavors.

> The UN should expand the Office of the UN High Commissioner for Human Rights' regional and country field presence and significantly raise financial support for priority human rights activities.

The UN Secretary-General should exercise his or her power under Article 99 of the UN Charter to raise human rights issues for consideration by the Security Council whenever advised to do so by the High Commissioner for Human Rights, the Special Procedures of the Human Rights Council, or the heads of the human rights components of UN peace missions.

The permanent members of the UN Security Council should voluntarily suspend their veto rights in situations involving mass atrocities.

The UN should consider ways in which new forms of technology can amplify human rights accountability.

National and regional legal systems

The judiciary has a pivotal role to play in upholding human rights. Only an independent judiciary can render justice impartially on the basis of law, thereby assuring the rights and fundamental freedoms of the individual. On this basis:

The international community must redouble its resolve to safeguard and enhance the independence and effectiveness of judiciaries worldwide, in line with existing international principles of the rule of law.

The international community should aim to bolster the role of existing regional human rights courts and also encourage the development of new regional human rights courts by the League of Arab States and in Asia and the Pacific. All UN Member States should agree to submit themselves to the authority of international tribunals whose jurisdiction can appropriately – geographically or otherwise – be extended to them.

At the global level, the UN should consider the creation of a World Human Rights Court, consistent with the principle of complementarity.

Non-governmental organizations

Non-governmental organizations play a frontline role in highlighting the importance of the rights protected in the UDHR, in drawing attention to shortcomings in their implementation, and in naming and shaming governments that are guilty of violations or of failing to protect their citizens from human rights abuses. *In light of this, it is especially important that states make reasonable accommodation for NGOs aiming to promote, protect, and investigate violations of human rights.*

Human rights education

Human rights education also has an indispensable role to play. Fostering a universal culture of human rights among all individuals and institutions through transformative human rights education "from the bottom-up" can add important impetus to the adoption and enforcement of legal standards by governments "from the top-down." *The Commission calls on all governments, international organizations, and NGOs to encourage and support transformative human rights education.*

Sovereignty

The era of human rights that was initiated by the UDHR has disposed of any notion of state sovereignty that purports to insulate states from external criticism of internal rights violations. One principle the UDHR represents, and rightly so, is that human rights in every country are the world's business. *The Commission wishes to affirm: first, that countries may not misuse their national sovereignty as an excuse for insulating themselves from external pressure on human rights; and second, that it is legitimate for states to raise human rights issues in conducting foreign relations.*

The international community needs a toolkit of governmental and multilateral responses to rights violations that is more legitimate and more sophisticated than we have today, and which relies on mechanisms other than the use of force. There are many instruments of change used: some widely acknowledged, like trade sanctions; some far less recognized, such as human rights "name and shame" mechanisms; and others perhaps less clearly articulated, such as providing shelter to migrants fleeing from neighboring countries in times of great distress. We recommend that a study be undertaken of what governments do when they genuinely want to seek to change another government's behavior, and what governments are susceptible to in terms of real world pressures on human rights.

The Commission supports the concept of the Responsibility to Protect (*RtoP*) governing the process of humanitarian intervention. However, intervention under the auspices of RtoP will be far from regular and will be appropriate only in the case of egregious and widespread human rights violations. The violation of rights, the erosion of rights, or the failure to fulfill rights are matters of concern, even when they are not widespread. Any time a violation occurs – which may affect one person or one thousand – we must take notice. Underpinning this imperative is the principle that the violation of the rights of anyone is the concern of everyone.

Human Rights and a Global Ethic

The promulgation of the UDHR in 1948 made a difference in how people saw their place in the world and their relations with their state and with each other. This is in itself a valuable contribution, quite apart from the securing of the rights actually listed in the document. Over the decades since 1948, the UDHR has provided the rudiments of a "common conscience" for humanity. In the words of Immanuel Kant, a violation of rights in any place is now felt all around the world. The international community is continuing to build on this, and the UDHR should be regarded as one of the pillars of an emerging global ethic for our increasingly interdependent world.

Preamble

Across the ages, people of different religions, civilizations, and political orders have advanced the ideal that each human being has moral ties and responsibilities to all others. And for three quarters of a century and more, in a world increasingly and globally interconnected, the human family has witnessed new and path-breaking initiatives to articulate and expand the summons of this ideal. Among the most vital and powerful of these endeavors is the 1948 Universal Declaration of Human Rights. From the start, endorsed and adopted by most Member States of the United Nations, the Declaration has been a beacon and a standard, its influence both wide and deep. It is a living document that demands renewed recognition and speaks urgently to the issues of today – even though states and others may repeatedly flout or fall short of the rights and norms it expresses.

We, the members of the Global Citizenship Commission, undertook our exploration of the Declaration, its legacy, and its promise with open minds. We were determined to learn from one another, with our distinct beliefs and our disparate places of origin, and ready to account for the weaknesses as well as the strengths of the Declaration and the modern human rights system for which it is a life force. We have discovered in our multinational collaboration that working together to reflect on the UDHR and its writ, its reach, and its impact has reaffirmed our faith in its stirring invocation of "the inherent dignity and of the equal and inalienable rights of all members of the human family" as "the foundation of freedom, justice and peace in the world […]" There is much more to be done to fully secure the rights and more effectively

  http://dx.doi.org/10.11647/OBP.0091.05

carry out the responsibilities that are essential to the work of making real the ideals of the UDHR. Hideous and systemic human rights abuses continue to be perpetrated at an alarming rate across the world. Sadly, too many people, so many of them in authority, are hostile to human rights or indifferent to their claims – or willing to devalue them as secondary issues. This makes it all the more imperative to reassert our firm belief in the call of the UDHR as a central mission for all the world.

Most of this report involves a detailed discussion of the UDHR and its enduring relevance for today. But we begin by elaborating the sense of global community and global ethics in which both the Declaration and our discussions are grounded.

The idea that every human being is part of a seamless human fabric, a single global community, bound by moral ties to every other human being, is as ancient as recorded history. Confucius, born in the sixth century BCE in Lu State, China, conceived of "all under heaven" as the widest span of moral concern; two centuries later, Diogenes of Sinope, a Greek settlement on the southern coast of the Black Sea, declared that he was a citizen of the cosmos, of the entire earth. The Abrahamic faiths – Judaism, Christianity and Islam – are all rooted in the concept that every human being is the creation of a loving God who cares for us and commands us to care for one another. Buddhism and Hinduism enshrine the interconnectedness of all creatures, the view of a shared humanity is voiced in the Southern African notion of Ubuntu, and the same fundamental insight is found in the traditions of peoples on every continent. There is, in short, a global understanding that, in the truest sense, we are a single human family.

None of these separate traditions, however, proposed a commitment to a global community resting on the creation of a single world government. And neither do we. Historically, each held that moral duties were strongest toward those to whom we were closest. As concern moved out from friends and families, moral obligations were attenuated. There were special obligations to those with whom we shared a state, but there were still real and significant obligations to others with whom we did not. This duty to care is the basis for citizenship – local or global.

The idea of global citizenship does not, then, exclude citizenship in a nation or state, or membership in a family or a local community.

Indeed, it presupposes that we have significant moral connections at all three levels. As a Commission on Global Citizenship, our charge has been to reflect on what it is for each of us to be members of a global community and, in particular, what each of us owes to all others everywhere. But recognizing that we are all members of a single human community – citizens, as Diogenes put it, of the entire earth – is not just a matter of articulating rights and duties. It involves approaching each other with an attitude of respect and concern, treating each human being as someone who seeks and deserves to live a life of dignity, a life imbued with significance. For global citizenship to have practical meaning, we believe it is indispensable for us to come to a common appreciation of these basic ideas.

The need for a shared comprehension of our moral connections has become more and more pressing in the past century as the world has become more and more interdependent. Goods, money, diseases, pollutants, and ideas: all move across the globe more swiftly and sweepingly than ever, whether by ship or by plane, whether in the currents of the oceans and the atmosphere or electronically through the revolutionary media of our time, including, of course, the World Wide Web. Our ecological interconnections – through climate change and global epidemics, for example – require us each to join together to overcome challenges that have an impact on us all, and on the prospects of generations yet unborn. Global economic realities, and especially the persistence of extreme poverty, confront us with problems that are practical as well as moral challenges, which we can only meet and master in common cause.

In the decades since the Second World War, the UDHR stands as a monumental embodiment of that ancient idea that we all belong to a single global community and that all of us must do our part to ensure that every human being can live a life of dignity. With the endorsement of the nations of the world, the Declaration expressed the idea of the human family as a globally shared ideal. Article 1 speaks to the first principle that "all human beings are born free and equal in dignity and rights." Article 2 holds that "everyone is entitled to all the rights and freedoms set forth in this Declaration" without exception.

The notion of global citizenship can be empowering to every individual in the world, particularly when those suffering learn of its attachment to a set of basic human rights that are far more than they could have imagined. For this reason, we decided that exploring the continuing role and relevance of the UDHR was the best starting point for developing a common contemporary understanding of the meaning of global citizenship. That ambition is the guiding purpose of this report.

1. The Long and Influential Life of the Universal Declaration of Human Rights

1.1 History of the UDHR

The Universal Declaration of Human Rights emerged from the ashes of the Second World War. With the end of the conflict, and the creation of the United Nations, the international community vowed never again to abide the unspeakable atrocities the world had just witnessed. So the leaders of the world decided to amplify the UN Charter by enshrining and encouraging guarantees for the rights of human beings everywhere.

In 1946, as part of the preliminary work of drafting the Declaration, under the auspices of UNESCO, Jacques Maritain assembled a Philosophers' Committee to identify key theoretical issues in framing a charter of rights for all peoples and all nations. The work of the Philosophers' Committee then moved to the UN Commission on Human Rights. At its first session in January 1947, the Commission authorized its members to formulate what it termed "a preliminary draft international bill of human rights." Later the work was taken over by a formal drafting committee, consisting of members of the Commission from eight states. The Commission on Human Rights comprised 18 members from various political, cultural, and religious backgrounds. Eleanor Roosevelt, the widow of President Franklin D.

          http://dx.doi.org/10.11647/OBP.0091.06

Roosevelt, chaired the Commission. It also included René Cassin of France, who composed the first draft of the declaration; Commission Rapporteur Charles Malik of Lebanon; Vice-Chairman Peng Chung Chang of China; and John Humphrey of Canada, Director of the UN's Human Rights Division, who prepared the Declaration's blueprint.

The Commission had to resolve issues of fundamental importance. First, it concluded that the right mission was to develop a declaration, rather than a treaty. The Commission's view was that the declaration should be relatively short, inspirational, energizing, and broadly accessible to peoples everywhere: the defining document of an international bill of human rights. It also decided that the declaration should encompass both civil and political rights, on the one hand, and social and economic rights, on the other.

Cassin handed his draft of the declaration to a meeting of the Commission on Human Rights in Geneva. Thus this version, which was sent to all UN Member States for comment, became known as the "Geneva draft." The Commission revised the Geneva draft to reflect the replies it had received from Member States, before submitting it to the General Assembly. The General Assembly in turn scrutinized the document between September and December of 1948, with over 50 Member States voting a total of 1,400 times on practically every clause and virtually every word of the text. By its resolution 217 A (III) of 10 December 1948, the General Assembly, meeting in Paris, voted to adopt the UDHR with eight nations abstaining but none dissenting.[1] It was an historic moment, and the General Assembly called upon all Member States to publicize the text of the Declaration and "to cause it to be disseminated, displayed, read, and expounded principally in schools

---

1   The following 48 countries voted in favor of the Declaration: Afghanistan, Argentina, Australia, Belgium, Bolivia, Brazil, Burma, Canada, Chile, China, Colombia, Costa Rica, Cuba, Denmark, Dominican Republic, Ecuador, Egypt, El Salvador, Ethiopia, France, Greece, Guatemala, Haiti, Iceland, India, Iran, Iraq, Lebanon, Liberia, Luxembourg, Mexico, Netherlands, New Zealand, Nicaragua, Norway, Pakistan, Panama, Paraguay, Peru, Philippines, Siam, Sweden, Syria, Turkey, United Kingdom, United States, Uruguay, and Venezuela. The following eight countries abstained: the Soviet Union, Ukrainian SSR, Byelorussian SSR, People's Federal Republic of Yugoslavia, People's Republic of Poland, Union of South Africa, Czechoslovakia, and the Kingdom of Saudi Arabia. Honduras and Yemen – both members of the UN at the time – failed to vote or abstain.

and other educational institutions, without distinction based on the political status of countries or territories."

The UDHR formed the basis for two covenants which were adopted by the General Assembly in 1966: the International Covenant on Civil and Political Rights and the International Covenant on Economic, Social and Cultural Rights. These Covenants have binding status in international law. The Declaration and the Covenants are collectively known as the "International Bill of Human Rights."

Today, the Universal Declaration, translated into 350 languages, is the best-known and most often cited human rights document on Earth. By setting out, for the first time, fundamental rights to be universally protected, it is a milestone in the history of human interactions and the cause of human rights.

1.2 Affirming and protecting the UDHR

Given that the UDHR is best understood as a living enterprise that challenges each new generation to new actions to fulfill and extend its writ, the aim of the Commission has been to assess what needs to be understood and undertaken in the twenty-first century to realize the high ideals of the UDHR, and to reinforce its status as a foundational document of global citizenship. Therefore, the Commission not only celebrates the framers of the Declaration – together with all those who have worked so hard over the years to sustain it – but, in that spirit, we also set forth issues on which we believe the international community should focus in renewing the 1948 enterprise for our day and generation.

So the Commission both affirms the UDHR and seeks to further recognition and respect for human rights for all citizens of the world, in the life and light of the twenty-first century. The intention of our report is not to rewrite or revise the UDHR. Rather, what we have learned and share here should be regarded as an analytical commentary that reflects changed circumstances and progress in our moral thought since the first days of the Declaration. The report further observes that individuals, states, and other entities each and all have a common duty to ensure recognition of human rights and accept responsibility to secure them.

1.3 The changing context

The social, political, and legal environment has been transformed since 1948. It is impossible to list all the changes, but many are of sweeping and particular importance. Decolonization, the breakup of old empires, and the emergence of new states mean that there are 193 UN Member States today, compared to the 58 of 1948. Some would say that states have risen and then declined in importance since 1948. Certainly in recent years the growth in the number of states has been matched by the growth of new centers of authority, and by an increase in the power of non-state actors.

Our global interdependence now plays a central and often contentious role: globalization is a major phenomenon in economics and trade as well as politics, culture, communications, and technology. International institutions have far greater sway in world affairs than they did in 1948, both those associated with the United Nations itself and those that hold an independent status. There is more and more awareness too of global challenges such as climate change. New patterns of life and economic development have emerged, as have new patterns of migration and inequality.

In 1948, the memory of the Second World War was fresh in everyone's minds. Since then new forms of conflict have emerged: the Cold War dominated the period between the 1950s and 1980s; today armed conflict frequently involves non-state actors; and there is the prolonged struggle against terrorism. Along with such new forms of conflict have come new formulations of international responsibilities such as the Responsibility to Protect.

We have been able to reconsider the UDHR after 70 years not only in light of these changed circumstances, but also in the context of the undeniable truth that global interconnectedness and dependence have diminished our moral distance from each other.

1.4 The enduring relevance of the UDHR

One of the tasks of the Commission is to apply the abstract language of the Declaration to the reality of the twenty-first century. The question we should ask is not what the framers of the UDHR would have thought about a particular issue in 1948. Instead, the question is what we should think now, in the world of today, animated by the same principles that animated the framers then.

The UDHR purports to offer a shared basis for comprehending both the idea of human rights itself and the array of human rights that the idea implies. Specifically, the Declaration presents what the Preamble calls a "common understanding" of human rights and represents what the Proclamation Clause calls "a common standard of achievement for all peoples and all nations." We believe that the assertion of a "common understanding" of human rights and "a common standard of achievement for all peoples and all nations" was a vital step in 1948 and we believe it remains equally vital in the twenty-first century.

Part of that vitality is that the clauses of the UDHR provide a tangible focus of orientation; so that when people debate human rights there is less chance of talking in circles or at cross-purposes. Even if people disagree with the UDHR's formulations, the formulations nevertheless help to structure their disagreements and arguments. More than that, however, the Declaration embodies a set of common expectations for the dealings of nations and peoples with one another, so far as the proper treatment of individuals is concerned. It makes apparent that this is a subject on which firm, explicit, and reasonably clear standards have been publicly laid down. Having this common point of reference has been of immeasurable political importance in both large-scale and small-scale campaigns to protect peoples and individuals from abuses. Here we have in mind large-scale campaigns like the articulation of human rights in the Helsinki movement from 1975, as well as small-scale, even village-level, campaigns in various parts of the world.

Most of all, the UDHR gives substance to the idea that there actually is such a thing as a "common conscience" for mankind. One of the most fundamental things that human rights declarations and human rights law can do is to establish certain taboos around serious abuses and violations. Quite apart from enforcement, this is a matter of culture and positive morality. It is essential that those who abuse individuals should recognize that there is something called "human rights" that they are violating, and that both those who suffer abuses and those who observe them should have a common and publicly recognized vocabulary in which to express denunciation of this conduct and to organize resistance against it.

So we believe the UDHR has been and is an unprecedented educational and cultural force, making people conversant with the idea of human rights, providing a widely accepted text enumerating those rights, and delivering an articulate focus for what might otherwise be timid and inarticulate concerns. The UDHR in 1948 laid the foundation for our modern culture of human rights. Now, as distinct from 1948, the document functions in a world that by and large takes human rights seriously, a world in which the idea and culture of human rights are pervasive though implementation falls far short of the ideals, a world in which the idea of human rights can no longer be dismissed as simply aspirational and unworldly. In short, the UDHR has had a shaping influence on the world in which it now operates.

1.5 Legal status

The UDHR was originally formulated as "soft law;" it was aspirational, not legally binding. Since its adoption, however, the UDHR has been complemented by the two covenants that are legally binding on the nations that have signed and ratified them: the International Covenant on Civil and Political Rights, which came into force in 1976 and has been ratified by 168 nations; and the International Covenant on Economic, Social and Cultural Rights, which also came into force in 1976 and has been ratified by 164 nations. Further, many provisions of the UDHR are also now part of customary international law. There are additional conventions on particular human rights concerns, such as the International Convention on the Elimination of All Forms of Racial Discrimination (*ICERD*), the Convention on the Elimination of All Forms of Discrimination Against Women (*CEDAW*), the Convention Against Torture and Other Cruel, Inhuman or Degrading Treatment or Punishment (*CAT*), the Convention on the Rights of the Child (*CRC*), and the Convention on the Rights of Persons with Disabilities (*CRPD*).

The International Bill of Human Rights is matched in many cases by the rights provisions of national constitutions, charters, and bills of rights. Some of these, like the U.S. Bill of Rights, predate the UDHR by decades or centuries. Others, including the constitutions of some of the newest countries in the world, have been cast in the image of the

International Bill of Human Rights, directly or indirectly adopting ideas and formulations from these international instruments. In this way the UDHR provides a template for national law-making, and forges a continuum between the international protection of human rights and their protection under public law in particular countries. Such international and national instruments are complemented by regional treaties – principally the African Charter on Human and Peoples' Rights, the American Convention on Human Rights, and the European Convention on Human Rights.

In reality, most of the legal work to secure human rights and vindicate them in the face of violations is conducted under the auspices of national and regional law and practice. This will continue to be the ordinary mode of implementation in the twenty-first century, and one of the roles of international declarations like the UDHR and the Covenants should be to serve as a model for structuring local constitutional and legislative arrangements.

1.6 Foundational principles

The Declaration does not clearly indicate the reasons for enumerating the particular rights it mentions, nor does it articulate the philosophical ideas upon which these rights are predicated. However, the Commission believes that the UDHR's emphasis on the principle of human dignity is the keystone. The Preamble enunciates the principle: "recognition of the inherent dignity and of the equal and inalienable rights of all members of the human family is the foundation of freedom, justice and peace in the world." The United Nations clause says that the Member States have "reaffirmed their faith in fundamental human rights, in the dignity and worth of the human person." And Article 1 reaffirms the ideal that "all human beings are born free and equal in dignity and rights."

In the Covenants, dignity is also cited as a way of determining what a particular right entails. For example, Article 10(1) of the ICCPR says: "All persons deprived of their liberty shall be treated with […] respect for the inherent dignity of the human person," and Article 13(1) of the ICESCR recognizes a right to education and provides that "education shall be directed to the full development of the human personality and the sense of its dignity." There is a reference of this kind in the UDHR's conditions of work provision, Article 23, which asserts, among other things, that "everyone who works has the right to just and favourable remuneration ensuring for himself and his family an existence worthy of human dignity."

Dignity is not defined in the UDHR or in any of the human rights documents that repeatedly invoke it. But it is clear that human dignity is a special status that accrues to all people on account of the inherent features of their human being, their human potential, and their human qualities and capacities. As a status dignity implies a number of important rights and responsibilities; it generates a basis on which people can exact respect for themselves from others; it is an equal status; and it inheres in people by virtue of their humanity as such, irrespective of merit or demerit.

Human dignity is often cited as a value or principle associated integrally and perhaps foundationally with human rights. The Preamble to the ICCPR announces this specifically, "recognizing that these rights derive from the inherent dignity of the human person." A number of national constitutions also make human dignity the centerpiece of their bills or charters of fundamental rights. These include the South African Constitution (Articles 1, 7, and 10), the Chinese Constitution (Article 38), the Basic Law of Germany (Article 1.1), and many others.

1.7 Universality

Our report makes a number of claims about what ought to count as a human right: for example, that it is every human being's right not to be enslaved, and that it is every human being's right to marry and found a family. How are such claims to be understood? Specifically, are they put forward as principles that everyone ought to accept regardless of his or her religion or cultural tradition, or are they meant merely to reflect the values of a particular segment of the human population?

To say that freedom from enslavement is a human right is not merely to express a preference for living in a world in which no one is enslaved. It is also not merely to say that freedom from slavery is an ideal to which we happen to subscribe but that others are free to reject in favor of a competing ideal. It is to say that enslaving people deprives them of a condition of life to which they are *entitled* inalienably as a result of being human. There is no way to understand this claim as simply the expression of a mere preference; it is put forward and urged on everybody as a matter of principle.

But how is such a principled commitment to avoid coming across as disrespectful towards the potentially vast number of human beings who may disagree with a particular human rights claim? The claim about slavery may no longer be controversial in our time; but the claim about marriage, for example, is an occasion for much controversy with different interpretations both advanced and rejected by large numbers of people around the globe. If we adopt a particular view, are we not in danger of just imposing our own values on others, without consideration of their opposing points of view?

We do not think so. First, when a claim, any claim, is put forward as true, that is not the same thing as saying that it is put forward as *certain*, or *infallible*, or *not open to rational discussion*. The claim needs to be backed up with reasons and arguments, and any reasons and arguments on the other side need to be listened to, considered, and answered. We have sought to arrive at the moral conclusions about human rights that seem to us most justified by what we judge to be the best moral thinking of our time. However, we remain entirely sensitive to the possibility that we have fallen short and invite anyone who disagrees with our conclusions to assert and argue the countervailing considerations.

Second, many expressions of human rights – including those of the UDHR – allow for a certain amount of contextual variation. For example, the UDHR is emphatic in Articles 10 and 11 that people have the right to due process when they are accused of any crime, but the legal systems of the world vary in their procedural arrangements and, within broad limits, the UDHR respects such variations.

Finally, the formulations of human rights declarations are often vague and abstract, and they leave certain issues unsettled and open to interpretation. These are often matters of good-faith disagreement within particular countries and between particular countries. So, for example, some countries may regard corporal punishment as consistent in principle with Article 5 (the anti-torture provision) while other countries emphatically reject this. Similarly, some countries may see the disenfranchisement of convicted prisoners as consistent with Article 21 (the democracy provision) while others will disagree. This openness of the UDHR is one of its great virtues. It does not preclude the emergence of a checkerboard of interpretations around the world of its various provisions, reflecting what European human rights lawyers call a "margin of appreciation" for discrete national practices and sensibilities. The room for interpretation is not unlimited, but the provisions of the Declaration were not intended to settle every last detail.

1.8 Interconnectivity of rights

It was no doubt important to divide the binding human rights instruments into two separate covenants – the ICCPR and ICESCR – if only to secure ratification of at least one of these (e.g., the ICCPR by the United States or the ICESCR by China) in circumstances where the ratification of the other was not possible. But the unity of the UDHR in this respect – the fact that it combines civil, political, economic, social, and cultural rights in a single declaration with a single preamble – is critical.

The UDHR does not explicitly commit itself to any thesis of the indivisibility of human rights. But implicitly it conveys the impression that the values that underpin, for example, the free expression provision, the anti-torture provision, and the democracy provision are grounded in the same way and stand upon the same foundation as the values that underpin the social security provision, the conditions of work provision, and the standard of living provision. Not everyone is convinced of this, of course, but we think it was an appropriate stance to take in drafting the UDHR.

Although the rights set out in the UDHR are presented as a list – line item by line item – it is imperative to acknowledge the interconnectivity of these rights. We should understand the Declaration as an implicit expression of the interconnections, overlaps, and mutual reinforcement between rights. By way of illustration, both Article 4 (the anti-slavery provision) and Article 16 (the marriage and family provision) are relevant to child marriage.

2. The Evolving Understanding of Rights

Globalization has changed the terms of interaction in global life, and it has created space both for implicit extensions of and explicit additions to the content of human rights doctrine. We recall that since 1948 there have been many other substantive human rights conventions that have addressed some of the issues we identify – including the rights of women, the rights of children, and the rights of the disabled. Nevertheless, it is important to recognize a number of rights that we think have come into clearer focus after 70 years and need more emphasis than they received in the Declaration. Some of these rights are mentioned in the UDHR, such as the rights of women, but we want to suggest that the language could have been more vivid in light of what we now know. Other rights, such as those related to sexual orientation, are not expressly addressed at all in the document, and involve a change in consciousness and concern since the UDHR was adopted. But it is arguable that even these can be understood as an elaboration of rights to personal freedom or autonomy that are in fact clearly affirmed in the Declaration.

The suggestions below are preliminary and non-exhaustive, and many of them are controversial. We view our role as initiating a conversation on the challenges raised by particular issues, rather than trying to legislate definitively on the content of particular rights. Our aim is not to rewrite the Declaration or suggest amendments to it. Instead the Commission wishes to pay tribute to the enduring power of the original document, and draw attention to new issues that reflect our understanding of human rights today.

       http://dx.doi.org/10.11647/OBP.0091.07

2.1 Rights of members of specific groups

a. The rights of women

A large part of the world condones the systemic violation of the human rights of women on a daily basis – whether directly in the form of domestic violence, female genital cutting, forced marriage, and other forms of oppression, or indirectly in the way women have to bear the consequences of extreme poverty and a lack of access to healthcare and to safe water and sanitation. These indirect impacts on the rights of women also include, for example, traditional systems of land ownership and inheritance, economies that fail to ensure women can have enough income to support a decent standard of life from birth to old age, systems of family law that make it impossible for women to leave situations of violence, and attitudes with respect to employment that result in women being paid less for the same work and working disproportionately in informal and insecure sectors.

The Commission wishes to highlight that the framers of the Declaration recognized in 1948 that gender equality was essential. Article 2 of the UDHR expressly held that "everyone is entitled to all the rights and freedoms set forth in this Declaration, without distinction of any kind, such as [...] sex." In light of the widespread human rights violations perpetrated against women around the Earth in the subsequent 70 years, it is important to reaffirm without qualification that the grounding of the UDHR in human dignity requires that all people – including all women – enjoy the rights set out in the UDHR, including the right to education, the right to freedom of peaceful assembly and association, the right to equal employment opportunities, the right to marry only with free and full consent, and the right to be free from torture and cruel, inhuman, or degrading treatment.[1] Women's rights, including all rights recognized in the ICCPR and CEDAW, must be recognized as real and women must be respected by governments everywhere in

---

[1]   The use of gender-specific language and assumptions in the UDHR – such as the language of "human brotherhood" in Article 1 and the implication in Article 23(3) that it is men who work and provide subsistence for a family – is a function of the time and should not be read as discriminatory.

the world as equal to men – irrespective of religions and cultures. Our point is that formal equality is not sufficient: as recognized by Goal 5 of the Sustainable Development Goals, there is a need to actually *achieve* gender equality and empower all women and girls. It is crucial to give attention to the gender impacts of systems and attitudes that are apparently "gender-blind." The UDHR must be read in a way that highlights the specific impact upon women of certain abuses, certain attitudes, and certain forms of neglect.

b. The rights of children

The UDHR does not expressly recognize the rights of children. In fact, it was not until the adoption of the CRC in 1989 that the rights of the world's youngest were explicitly acknowledged by an international treaty. The CRC articulated, for the first time, that children possess innate rights equal to those of adults: rights to health, to education, to protection, and to equal opportunity.

Nonetheless, a number of provisions in the UDHR are relevant to the rights of children. Article 25, the standard of living provision, recognizes that children are "entitled to special care and assistance." Article 26 of the Declaration sets out the right to education. In fact, the education section is one of the most detailed provisions of the UDHR. And Article 16(1) of the UDHR, the marriage and family provision, reads: "Men and women of full age, without limitation due to race, nationality or religion, have the right to marry and to found a family." It is clear that the right of parents to found and raise a family is not only a right – it is also a responsibility. Consequently, the rights of children are not just rights in relation to governments: they are, in the first instance, rights in relation to their parents.

There are different kinds of incentives for upholding the rights of children in different parts of the world. In some cases, both the child's parents and the government keep their eyes closed to violations. Thus, in addition to recognizing the obligations of parents and governments, we should also acknowledge the responsibilities of the community at large, including non-governmental organizations (**NGOs**).

No account of the rights of children would be complete without highlighting slavery. Children make up a substantial portion of the 35.8

million people that Walk Free estimates are enslaved around the world. While measuring this hidden crime is difficult, based on World Bank age distribution data and the Global Slavery Index, there are currently an estimated 8.7 million children in slavery. Slavery is expressly prohibited by Article 4 of the Declaration: "No one shall be held in slavery or servitude; slavery and the slave trade shall be prohibited in all their forms."[2]

The Commission also considered the issue of child marriage specifically. Article 16(2) of the Declaration says: "Marriage shall be entered into only with the free and full consent of the intending spouses." However, in certain parts of the world, "free and full consent" is often assumed based on custom, culture, or tradition. And the assertion is frequently made that this is an instance of competing rights: the right of a child to marry freely, against the right to freedom of culture or freedom of religion. Indeed, there is a strong linkage between the existence of dual or parallel legal systems within a country and the prevalence of child, early, and forced marriages. While most national laws prohibit child, early, and forced marriages, in those countries where customary, tribal, or religious laws are a powerful civil force, they are sometimes abused to compromise or undermine national laws regulating marriage. These laws expose children to child marriage, and potentially condemn them to a life of poverty and violence.

Custom, culture, and tradition may not legitimately dispense with the requirement of explicit individual consent. We insist that the rights of children (like those of women) can never properly be denied in the name of particular beliefs or cultures. A simple, positive statement should be made to young people that "you do not have to get married unless you want to." On this view, the greatest hope for fulfilment of the Declaration is that the people, families, and communities most

---

2   It is worth noting that Article 1(d) of the UN Supplementary Convention on the Abolition of Slavery states that "any institution or practice whereby a child or young person under the age of 18 years, is delivered by either or both of his natural parents or by his guardian to another person, whether for reward or not, with a view to the exploitation of the child or young person or of his labour" is an institution or practice similar to slavery.

susceptible to human rights abuses begin to understand the Declaration, grasp it, and use it as their shield.

The Commission wishes to advance a number of proposals that would strengthen the protection of children's rights in the twenty-first century. At the international level, we propose the creation of a Children's Court, with the power to receive and adjudicate petitions from children and their representatives on violations of the CRC, issue legally binding judgments, and investigate areas of concern including child labor, child slavery, and child marriage.[3] The Commission also calls for the International Criminal Court to investigate and prosecute crimes against children within its remit to the full extent of the law. Further, we recommend that the UN Security Council convene a "Children's Council" – an annual debate on children's rights, building on its existing review of the issue of children in armed conflict. At the national level, the Commission urges states to create accessible complaint mechanisms for the resolution of violations of the rights of children, and to consider establishing a Youth Parliament, Children's Commissioner, and dedicated Children's Budget. We believe that these measures can play a vital role in realizing the rights articulated in the CRC.

c. The rights of the disabled, including the profoundly disabled

The right to equality, enshrined in the UDHR, is as relevant to people with disabilities as it is to any other members of society. The UDHR makes no mention of human disability, apart from an oblique mention in Article 25, which cites a person's inability to secure subsistence "in

---

3   Children from countries that have ratified the Third Optional Protocol to the CRC can submit a complaint to the Committee on the Rights of the Child if their rights under the Convention, or its two earlier Optional Protocols, have been violated by the state and when all domestic remedies have been exhausted. To date, however, only 24 states have ratified the Third Optional Protocol, and many of those states have failed to adequately educate the public as to its existence. Further, this form of redress is political, rather than legal, and decisions made by the Committee are non-binding.

circumstances beyond his control." However, in 2006, the UN adopted the Convention on the Rights of Persons with Disabilities, which represents a paradigm shift in the global movement from viewing persons with disabilities as "objects" of charity, medical treatment, and social protection towards viewing persons with disabilities as "subjects" with rights, who are capable of claiming those rights and making decisions for their lives based on their free and informed consent.

Speaking philosophically, disability may pose particular issues when humans lack the characteristics or capacities on which human dignity is usually grounded. And speaking practically, disability may require particular and if need be costly attention to the way in which rights are fulfilled. We believe it is vital to reaffirm the possession of human rights by all humans, including those suffering from disabilities.

Disability covers a wide range of human situations, with loss of part of one's capacities at one end (e.g., deafness, blindness, loss of limbs) ranging all the way through to a profound loss of cognitive capacity at the other. The Commission emphasizes the rights of people suffering from disabilities at each point on the spectrum, and the importance of taking reasonable measures to facilitate the exercise and fulfilment of such rights. Even when the disability is profound, we must respect the human lives and human needs of those who cannot participate with others on equal terms.

d. Rights related to sexual orientation

It is important to highlight two particular omissions of the UDHR with respect to sexual orientation: first, that sexual orientation and transgender status is not mentioned in Article 2 – the universality provision – as a category that cannot justify a restriction of rights; and second, that Article 16 – the marriage and family provision – does not explicitly establish rights for lesbian, gay, bisexual, and transgender (**LGBT**) people to marry and to found a family. The omissions are understandable, as a new normative context around sexual orientation and transgender status has only emerged in the past 20 years.

Nevertheless, the Commission wishes to address these omissions by affirming that: first, everyone is entitled to all the rights and freedoms enumerated in the UDHR without distinction based on sexual orientation or transgender status; second, Article 7, the non-discrimination provision, should be understood to prohibit discrimination on the grounds of sexual orientation or transgender status; and third, Article 16 protects the rights of LGBT people to marry and to found a family. There is no getting round the fact that the controversy around same-sex marriage is a human rights issue. There is a need to acknowledge it as such and debate it as such.

e. The rights of prisoners

Article 10 of the ICCPR establishes certain rights of prisoners that have developed as guiding norms of international human rights law. Some of these are specific, such as the segregation of juvenile from adult prisoners. Some are quite general, including the requirement that all persons deprived of their liberty shall be treated with humanity and with respect for the inherent dignity of the human person.

The rights of prisoners have become a particularly acute issue in recent years with the emergence of new forms of detention as part of the response to international terrorism. The Commission believes that Article 10 of the ICCPR was right to make explicit these principles, which are essential to a just penitentiary system and a necessary complement to Article 5 of the UDHR, which prohibits cruel, inhuman, or degrading treatment or punishment.

From a human rights point of view, the *scale* of incarceration may be an issue, as well as the conditions that people face when incarcerated. Indeed, many of the concerns about the role played by factors such as race and drugs in sustaining disproportionately high levels of prison populations in certain countries are human rights concerns.

Prisoners retain the bulk of their fundamental rights, with the exception of those rights directly affected by restrictions implicit in their incarceration. It remains debated whether rights such as the right to vote should be maintained by prisoners when they are incarcerated. The Commissioners accept that disagreement on this question may, depending on the content of the view, constitute reasonable disagreement. However, the right to vote should never be denied to people who have finished a custodial sentence on the basis of their having been convicted of an offense. The penalty for the crime is the custodial sentence itself. Beyond that, to deprive people of one of the fundamental democratic rights denies them the full citizenship to which all are entitled, and undermines the process of their social reintegration.

2.2 Rights of groups as such

Human rights are in the first instance rights of individuals. However, human communities, human peoples, and human families are also possessed of human rights, and recent developments in human rights law have made this plain.

Group rights are a difficult and controversial idea, but there is no doubt that some human communities are entitled to rights, whether conceived as the aggregate of members' individual rights or the rights of the group as a whole.

a. The right to national self-determination, including regional autonomy and subsidiarity

The UDHR makes no mention of national self-determination or the self-determination of peoples as a right. On the contrary, the UDHR still uses the language of colonialism, with Member States pledging to promote respect for human rights "among the peoples of territories under their jurisdiction." However, both the ICCPR and the ICESCR recognize the right of "all peoples" to self-determination by virtue of which they freely determine their political status and freely pursue their economic, social, and cultural development.

The omission of the right to self-determination from the UDHR is understandable, as the decolonization movement largely occurred after 1948 (and before the adoption of the ICCPR and ICESCR in 1966). Nonetheless, international recognition of this right emerged swiftly, and the Commission believes that the wording in the first Article of each of the Covenants was an essential addition to the International Bill of Human Rights. Admittedly, the definition of "peoples" remains controversial in many circumstances, but the formulations of the

Covenants point us to the fact that these controversies need to be worked out as human rights issues.

b. The rights of indigenous peoples

Particular attention needs to be paid to the situation of indigenous peoples: those who were the original inhabitants of lands impacted by imperial expansion and colonialism. More and more efforts are underway nationally and internationally to take the rights of indigenous peoples into account. The UDHR's emphasis on equality makes cultural protection a legitimate interest, and thereby provides a justification for such efforts.

c. Ethnic cleansing

Ethnic cleansing was of intense importance in 1948, and is a matter of grave concern today, as recognized by its inclusion in the Rome Statute of the International Criminal Court. It would be good for human rights declarations to embrace a clear and explicit understanding of ethnic cleansing as a grievous human rights abuse. It is important that human rights be understood not just for what they are, but also in the different modes in which they may be abused and violated, of which ethnic cleansing is one.

d. The rights of peoples prejudiced at the national or communal level by climate change

Climate change is a genuinely new issue, which has emerged in the last 20 to 25 years. There is no way it could have been envisaged in 1948. It is, however, urgent for the international community to address it in 2016. Climate change may well turn out to be the most consequential global challenge of the twenty-first century. It will reshape the concept of global citizenship in a number of regards, but the implications for human rights will be severe and should command the closest attention and thought among human rights advocates.

There are already, and there will be in future, massive implications for local and global economies, for human subsistence, and for migration. The impacts will not be felt evenly. For example, environmental migrants are often drawn from the most marginalized members of society, groups dependent on agriculture, populations in the least developed countries, in low-lying areas and coastal areas, and of course those impacted by national disasters. Increases in extreme weather events, the inundation of low-lying areas, and changes in patterns of weather affecting food production will all have a direct and also an indirect impact on people's rights as they are understood in the UDHR.

2.3 Rights related to other issues involving vital interests

a. Migration

The movement of people and peoples was an issue in 1948 and it is once again a pressing concern. The UDHR offers some resources for thinking about migration. Article 14, the asylum provision, provides that "everyone has the right to seek and to enjoy in other countries asylum from persecution." And Article 15 states that everyone has the right to a nationality and no one shall be arbitrarily deprived of his nationality nor denied the right to change his nationality.

Migration has become salient in new ways in our time. First, its scale has multiplied since 1948, with the wave of international migrants anticipated to surpass 250 million in 2015. Remittances from migrant workers play a significant role in economic development, with more than 400 billion USD a year flowing in this way to developing countries. Well-managed migration has been recognized as playing a decidedly positive role in economic development.

In 2015, conflict-related migration was at an all-time high, with worldwide displacement at the highest levels since records began. Much of this is the result of human rights violations in migrants' countries of origin. In 2015, the number of displaced people was expected to exceed 60 million, compared to 37.5 million a decade earlier. Over 5 million newly displaced people were reported in the first half of 2015, comparable to the 5.5 million newly displaced for the same period in 2014. Every day in 2014, 42,500 people became refugees, asylum seekers, or internally displaced.

Conflict-driven migration has high human and social costs. In 2015, over one million people arrived by sea in Europe, and more than 27,000 made crossings by sea in South-East Asia in the first half of the year, reflecting an explosion in the criminal trade of moving people from conflict zones for profit. We know this can have tragic consequences for some of the world's most vulnerable people: more than 46,000 migrants have died along migratory routes since 2000, and more than 3,770 died crossing the Mediterranean in 2015 alone. Worldwide, the total number of deaths across migratory routes in 2015 was 5,400.

Migration has enormous implications for the realization of human rights. While the UDHR applies to all persons irrespective of nationality or citizenship, in reality human rights are often inaccessible or denied to migrants. For example, refugees may be admitted to a country to seek safety but then denied the right to work. Migrant workers may be admitted to a country to work but legally prohibited from starting or joining trade unions. It must be recognized that those who move across state boundaries: retain their universal human rights and should be treated accordingly; have continuing rights in relation to their country of origin; have a right to security in transit, including freedom from forced or coerced movement; have a right to a fair and responsible process at borders and in all legal dealings with an actual or potential host country; and have a right to good reason for a refusal to allow entrance or settlement – refusal should not be based on ethnic, racial, religious, or other illegitimate discrimination.

While there are large-scale and varied international movements of people in the contemporary world, states often seek to restrict migration on economic, cultural, security, or other grounds. There is no consensus on the balance between rights to movement and the power of states to restrict it. However, given the current situation, there is an urgent need for the international community to strengthen the international refugee protection system. Perhaps we should be looking for a new international convention on refugees and migration. In any case, we endorse SDG target 10.7, which calls for states to "facilitate orderly, safe, regular and responsible migration and mobility of people, including through the implementation of planned and well-managed migration policies."

b. Statelessness

"Statelessness" arises when a person is deprived of a state and its legal system, which provides access to rights and remedies for their violation. Inasmuch as states have front-line responsibility for upholding the human rights of their citizens, stateless persons are deprived of the benefit of this responsibility. A person's legal right and ability to access human rights protections often depends on whether or not they are a national or citizen of the country they are in. This is about both lack of certainty in law and also prevailing social attitudes.

Statelessness is not a new issue. Article 15 of the UDHR upholds the right of every human being to a nationality. Nonetheless, there are still 10 million stateless people in the world today, over a third of whom are children. And during the past five years, 20 percent of all refugees resettled by the Office of the United Nations High Commissioner for Refugees (**UNHCR**) have also been stateless.[4]

Stateless people are deprived of rights that the majority of the global population takes for granted. Often they are excluded from cradle to grave – being denied a legal identity when they are born, access to education, health care, marriage, and job opportunities during their lifetime, and even the dignity of an official burial and death certificate when they die.

In the last three years there has been a positive trend toward resolving statelessness, as 26 states have acceded to the 1954 Convention relating

---

4   There are a number of causes of statelessness. Some countries do not recognize people from certain communities as citizens of that country. For instance, there are more than 800,000 Rohingya in Myanmar that have been refused nationality under the 1982 citizenship law, and many of the Bedouins of Kuwait are effectively stateless. Statelessness is also caused by the breakup of countries. More than two decades after the disintegration of the Soviet Union, over 600,000 people remain stateless. In addition, there are 27 countries in the world where women do not have the same rights as men to confer nationality on their children. So if you are a single mother of a child whose father is not known, you are unable to pass your nationality to your child. Finally, there are circumstances where bureaucratic difficulties in obtaining documentation such as birth certificates preclude people from accessing rights associated with nationality.

to the Status of Stateless Persons and the 1961 Convention on the Reduction of Statelessness. Still, only 82 countries in all have acceded to the 1954 Convention and only 60 countries have acceded to the 1961 Convention. In November 2014 the UNHCR launched a 10-Year Campaign to End Statelessness, and the Executive Committee of the High Commissioner's Programme approved a budget of 68 million USD for 2015. There is much more to be done to deal with statelessness, ensure that every birth is registered, and prevent gender and other forms of discrimination in nationality laws.

c. Administrative justice

The UDHR contains legality rights in Articles 8 to 11 but these mainly focus on criminal law. Given that administrative regulation is now pervasive, it is arguable that there should be a duty on bodies exercising governmental functions to act fairly, reasonably, and lawfully in decisions that materially affect an individual's rights and interests, and to ensure that individuals whose interests and livelihoods are affected by administrative decisions have a right to be heard prior to the decisions being made and a right to challenge them where appropriate.

d. Corruption

Corruption in the performance of state functions has been a problem since human governance began. Over the last 30 years there has been a rising awareness of the relevance of anti-corruption measures to the rule of law, state-building, and economic growth. The World Bank estimates that each year 20 billion USD to 40 billion USD, corresponding to 20 percent to 40 percent of official development assistance, is stolen through high level corruption from public budgets in developing countries and hidden overseas.[5] The flow on effects for access to rights are enormous.

The UN Convention Against Corruption, adopted in 2003, obliges State Parties to implement a wide and detailed range of anti-corruption

---

5   http://www.oecd.org/cleangovbiz/49693613.pdf

measures affecting their laws, institutions, and practices. These measures aim to promote the prevention, detection, and punishment of corruption, including domestic and foreign bribery, embezzlement, trading in influence, and money laundering, as well as the cooperation between State Parties on these matters.

Corruption is inextricably linked to the violation of an array of human rights, including the anti-slavery provision, the freedom of movement provision, and the legality provisions of Articles 8 to 11; moreover, people are wronged when they are denied equal access to governmental services as a result of corruption. This illustrates yet again the interconnectivity of rights and rights violations, described in section 1.8. There is a need and a duty for individuals, states, and other entities to recognize and respond to the human rights impact of governmental corruption, and to work to bring it to an end.

e. Privacy from state or corporate electronic surveillance

Article 12, the privacy and reputation provision, states that no one shall be subjected to arbitrary interference with his privacy.

In recent years there has been an exponential surge in the span and capacity of electronic communications, with concomitant opportunities for surveillance that can violate individuals' privacy rights. State surveillance can be an important law enforcement and national security intelligence-gathering tool when governed by strong rule of law requirements. But surveillance also poses risks, not only to privacy, but also to the freedoms of expression, association, and assembly, which increasingly are facilitated online and on mobile devices. Journalists, activists, government critics, and minority groups are especially vulnerable to abuse of states' surveillance powers. In addition, there are mounting concerns about threats to individual privacy from surveillance and commercially driven data collection by corporations.

These trends suggest to us that human rights documents need to cite new principles or new elaborations of old principles to balance the inevitable trade-offs that result from state or corporate electronic surveillance.

f. Access to the Internet and electronic communication on a global scale

A case can be made that access to the Internet and electronic communication is a human right. Some would object that a document like the UDHR aims to state core principles grounded in human dignity, and that the Internet is too recent and contingent a development to be recognized as the proper subject of a human right. Still, the provisions of the Declaration vary in the level of detail that they encompass – see, for example, the thorough language of Article 26, the education provision.

It is certainly important to understand that the specific rights set out in the Declaration extend to new technologies, including the Internet. This follows from our understanding of the UDHR as a living document. By way of illustration, the abstract language of Article 19 – read in the context of today – implies that the right to freedom of expression encompasses communication via the Internet. That article states that "everyone has the right to […] impart information and ideas through any media and regardless of frontiers."

Electronic communication, particularly through the Internet, enables the exercise of a range of other human rights. For example, social media provide a platform for people to exercise their Article 20 rights to peaceful assembly and association in circumstances where they otherwise could not do so.

g. Extreme poverty and deep economic inequality

The UDHR already enumerates a range of social and economic rights. It tends to state them in the affirmative: for example, the right to social security in Article 22 or the right to work in Article 23. Ever since 1948, however, there has been a contention that we should also maintain a focus on the conditions that continue to make social provision necessary. Two such conditions now merit particular attention: extreme poverty and deep economic inequality.

Economic inequality is defined by the gap between rich and poor, both nationally (within countries) and globally (between countries). Deep economic inequality refers to disparities that involve poverty on the one hand, and great riches on the other.[6] In general terms, poverty can be defined as an individual's or family's inability to meet basic needs such as food, shelter, clothing, water, sanitation, education, healthcare, nutrition, and access to communication. Extreme poverty refers to earning that lies below the international poverty line of 1.90 USD a day, as set by the World Bank.[7] The UDHR is not explicit about extreme poverty, but the recent SDG target to "by 2030, eradicate extreme poverty for all people everywhere" should be read as a continuation of the concerns stated in Article 25, the standard of living provision.

Extreme poverty clearly has direct implications for people's enjoyment and exercise of the rights they possess. And while deep inequality is not a violation of human rights *per se*, it is often associated with such violations, inasmuch as it has an impact upon access to political power and also makes discrimination more difficult to resist. Moreover, it is hard to maintain a sense of global citizenship in circumstances of such deep inequality that rich and poor cannot comprehend each other's lives, both within states and globally. Without such understanding, it is difficult for the rich to sympathize with the needs and predicaments of the poor, and difficult for them to see human dignity in the lives of the poor.

h. Healthcare

The UDHR makes a brief but powerful reference to healthcare in Article 25, which states that everyone has the right to a standard of living

---

6   Income inequality is on the rise, with the richest 10 percent earning up to 40 percent of total global income, while the poorest 10 percent earn only between 2 and 7 percent of total global income. In developing countries, inequality has increased by 11 percent if we take into account the growth of population. A significant majority of households in developing countries – more than 75 percent of the population – are living today in societies where income is more unequally distributed than it was in the 1990s. Evidence shows that, beyond a certain threshold, inequality harms growth and poverty reduction, the quality of relations in the public and political spheres, and individuals' sense of fulfillment and self-worth. SDG 10 is to "reduce inequality within and among countries."

7   According to the most recent estimates, in 2012, 896 million people lived on less than $1.90 a day. Just over 77.8 percent of the extremely poor lived in South Asia (309 million) and Sub-Saharan Africa (388.7 million). In addition, 147 million lived in East Asia and Pacific.

adequate for the health and well-being of himself and of his family, including food, clothing, housing, and medical care.

Access to health care, both in the form of public health provision in urban and rural areas, and in terms of disease and epidemic control, along with the availability of personal health care resources – these are all essential to health and life itself and must be recognized explicitly as rights. Article 12(1) of the ICESCR speaks of "the right of everyone to the enjoyment of the highest attainable standard of physical and mental health," and focuses particularly on the health of children. This should be read as an elaboration of the concerns embodied in Article 25.

i. A safe, clean, healthy, and sustainable environment

For obvious reasons, the international community is far more acutely aware of environmental threats today than it was in 1948. The international community has not yet recognized a human right to a decent and liveable environment *per se*. However, we believe that our understanding of human rights should embrace the right to a safe, clean, healthy, and sustainable environment, with a right of access for everyone to such elementary resources as clean air, clean water, and clean, safe, and sustainable energy.

We endorse the recent formulation of the Special Rapporteur[8] on human rights and the environment that "[a]ll human rights depend on the environment in which we live. A safe, clean, healthy and sustainable environment is integral to the full enjoyment of a wide range of human rights, including the rights to life, health, food, water and sanitation.

---

8   A Special Rapporteur is an individual working on behalf of the UN within the scope of the Special Procedures mechanisms, who bears a specific country or thematic mandate from the UN Human Rights Council. Special Rapporteurs undertake country visits; act on individual cases and concerns of a broader, structural nature by sending communications to states and others in which they bring alleged violations or abuses to their attention; conduct thematic studies and convene expert consultations; contribute to the development of international human rights standards, engage in advocacy, raise public awareness, and provide advice for technical cooperation.

Without a healthy environment, we are unable to fulfill our aspirations or even live at a level commensurate with minimum standards of human dignity. At the same time, protecting human rights helps to protect the environment. When people are able to learn about, and participate in, the decisions that affect them, they can help to ensure that those decisions respect their need for a sustainable environment." The very existence of the Special Rapporteur reflects the ability of the human rights system that has emerged since 1948 to respond to new challenges.

Concerns about a decent environment remind us that many rights need to be conceived of inter-generationally, and that our responsibilities must embrace the needs and predicaments of our children and grandchildren.

2.4 An open task

The UDHR left some vital questions unanswered and we have sought to point out some of the ways in which its lacunae have been or could be filled. But the task of identifying the rights we will need to guarantee in our progressively more interdependent world will remain open. The world is changing and humanity changes with it. As we confront the new realities produced by climate change, we may need to identify new rights necessary to protect fundamental human needs and interests; as new technologies develop in the life and information sciences, we may face challenges posed by the reshaping of our minds and bodies, through artificial intelligence or biotechnology. Perhaps, as science fiction writers and philosophers have suggested, we will one day have to consider the rights of beings we have created ourselves. But we believe that as the human community moves forward together to address such challenges, it will be able to build upon the firm foundations laid out in the UDHR.

3. Limitations and Derogations

3.1 Adequacy of Article 29 account of limitations

The second clause of Article 29 – "In the exercise of his rights and freedoms, everyone shall be subject only to such limitations as are determined by law solely for the purpose of securing due recognition and respect for the rights and freedoms of others and of meeting the just requirements of morality, public order and the general welfare in a democratic society" – assumes almost as a matter of course that some limitations on individual rights will be desirable or necessary. It was probably not the function of the UDHR to explain why this is the case. Its purpose has been much more to establish the rights that it proclaims than to vindicate any basis for their limitation. The Declaration as a whole should be read as the assertion of a strong presumption in favor of human rights, and Article 29(2) should be read as placing the burden of proof on anyone who seeks to limit them.

It is critical to recognize the force of Article 29(2)'s insistence that limitations cannot be particularistic or *ad hoc* but must be determined as a matter of law. In modern terms this would be associated with the idea of proportionality, a principle that has only been clearly articulated in more recent human rights law.[1] Similarly, the suggestion

---

1 The most common formulation of proportionality is as a three-part test, which asks: (1) Is the measure suitable to achieve a legitimate aim? (2) Is the measure necessary to achieve that aim or are less restrictive means available? (3) Does the measure nonetheless impose an excessive burden on the individual affected?

          http://dx.doi.org/10.11647/OBP.0091.08

that rights may be limited "for the purpose of securing due recognition and respect for the rights and freedoms of others" seems entirely sensible. Perhaps the number and breadth of the rights recognized in the UDHR mean that some conflict among them is inevitable. In articulating the basis on which such conflicts are justly resolved, it is important that all the right-holders in question be treated as equals. Further, limiting a right for the sake of other considerations should not be seen as disparaging that right or the underlying interest or liberty from which it flows in any particular case.

Nonetheless, the idea that the limitation of rights can be justified based on "morality, public order and the general welfare" strikes us as problematic. It is far too general. If "morality" is seen as the customs and mores of a particular society, then the UDHR will fail in its central purpose of creating a common understanding of human rights and the circumstances in which it is appropriate to limit these rights. (If "morality" means the principles of a correct universal moral code, by contrast, there is little hope of agreement as to its content.) And the reference to "the general welfare" as a ground of limitation seems to undercut the modern idea of rights as trumping utilitarian considerations. After all, the mere fact that the denial of a right would marginally increase national income provides no basis for such a denial. We realize that there are serious difficulties in defining clearly what bases for limiting a right, beyond a conflict with other rights, are permissible. The better way forward would be to develop shared understandings as to what reasons are *not* sufficient justifications for such limitations.

Article 29(2) does not mention resource limitations as a basis for limiting rights, especially social and economic rights. The only time such limitations are referred to in the UDHR is implicitly in Article 22, the general social security provision: "Everyone, as a member of society, has the right to social security and is entitled to realization, through national effort and international cooperation **and in accordance with the organization and resources of each State**, of the economic, social and cultural rights indispensable for his dignity and the free development of his personality [emphasis added]."

3.2 Derogation of rights in national or international emergencies

The question of rights in an emergency is distinct from the question of the balance between rights and the considerations mentioned in Article 29(2). The ICCPR recognizes this in the separate and extensive provision it makes for emergencies in its Article 4.[2] Here the ICCPR sets out the rules for derogations in times of emergency; it lays constraints on such derogations; and it identifies certain rights which may not be derogated even in times of emergency. The UDHR does none of this.

It is true that the UDHR initiated our thinking about human rights, and the issue of derogations (as set out in Article 4 of the ICCPR) is a product of a later phase in such thinking that we can now take advantage of. But the UDHR remains in and of itself something of crucial educational importance and a vital foundation of the global ethic of human rights. It is therefore a pity that it did not introduce the world to the idea of emergency derogations – and even more, to the idea that there are certain rights from which derogations may not be made, like the rights not to be tortured or enslaved. Such anti-derogation provisions establish the rights in question as more or less absolute.

The Commission also considered the increasing reliance in the modern world on long-term, continuous states of emergency as justifications for human rights derogations. One example is the U.S.-led

---

2   Article 4 of the ICCPR states:
    (1) In time of public emergency which threatens the life of the nation and the existence of which is officially proclaimed, the States Parties to the present Covenant may take measures derogating from their obligations under the present Covenant to the extent strictly required by the exigencies of the situation, provided that such measures are not inconsistent with their other obligations under international law and do not involve discrimination solely on the ground of race, color, sex, language, religion or social origin.
    (2) No derogation from articles 6, 7, 8 (paragraphs 1 and 2), 11, 15, 16, and 18 may be made under this provision.
    (3) Any State Party to the present Covenant availing itself of the right of derogation shall immediately inform the other States Parties to the present Covenant, through the intermediary of the Secretary-General of the United Nations, of the provisions from which it has derogated and of the reasons by which it was actuated. A further communication shall be made, through the same intermediary, on the date on which it terminates such derogation.

"War on Terror," which has now lasted for 14 years and has been invoked to justify such practices as drone strikes in Pakistan and the indefinite detention of inmates at Guantanamo Bay in Cuba. This challenge is not dealt with adequately by the formulations in Article 4 of the ICCPR, as they envisage relatively short-term, clearly demarcated emergencies. If there are to be long-term derogations of human rights, the international community must develop mechanisms to ensure that this process is not abused. In the Commission's view, the following standards should apply: first, derogations ought to be *publicly announced and publicly justified*, whenever possible, and organized in the context of a legislative framework that provides for *independent supervision and oversight*; second, the justification should substantiate that the derogations in question are the *minimum required to achieve the stated objectives*; third, suitable arrangements should be in place for the *supervision of detention*, including *procedural safeguards*; and fourth, derogations should be for a *fixed period*, with *renewal subject to the same conditions*.

The issue of long-term derogations of human rights should be the focus of discussion in relevant world bodies, such as the UN Human Rights Council, as well as across international civil society. The possibility of reaching international agreements on the relevant standards governing long-term derogations ought to be explored.

3.3 Regulation of the use of force

The UDHR was intended to operate in conjunction with the UN Charter's prohibition on the use of force.

Article 2(4) of the Charter provides that all UN Member States "shall refrain in their international relations from the threat or use of force against the territorial integrity or political independence of any state, or in any other manner inconsistent with the Purposes of the United Nations." It allowed only two exceptions to the prohibition on the use of force in international law: self-defence under Article 51, and military measures authorized by the UN Security Council in response to "any threat to the peace, breach of the peace or act of aggression."

Yet in recent years there have been military interventions that have been neither in self-defence nor authorized by the UN Security Council.

If the standards governing the use of force in the UN Charter are no longer effective, then the international community needs to create a new and more workable regime. Certainly we should understand that the UDHR and the UN Charter must operate together: a world in which war or the threat of war is endemic cannot be a world in which human rights are respected. The human rights community therefore has an interest in the workability of the UN Security Council's role being revisited. Any revision should maintain the fundamental restrictions on the use of force.

The rise and persistence of international terrorism have shown us that armed conflict is not confined to state organizations, and in many respects is not amenable in principle to the sort of rules and restrictions laid down in the UN Charter, which mainly envisage inter-state conflict. Much of the rethinking that is required affects the international law of armed conflict, and that is not our subject here. But the problem of international terrorism does raise a number of human rights issues – about surveillance, about detention of suspects, and about targeted killing. Since there appears to be no chance that these issues will abate soon, we need to address them on the basis that the circumstances giving rise to them have to be accepted for the time being as "the new normal." This does not mean that current tactics of surveillance, detention, and targeted killing should not be questioned. But in doing so human rights principles need to be given due consideration: these practices, and the necessities on which some would base them, must be addressed as permanent features of our human rights environment. Hard work needs to be done to create an architecture of values and principles, derived from current conceptions and the enduring foundations of human rights, that can deal coherently with these new features.

The Commission wishes to emphasize two further points. First, violations of human rights committed in the name of state security can actually facilitate international terrorism by marginalizing individuals and alienating key constituencies, thus generating community support for and complicity in the actions of violent extremists. To be effective and sustainable, therefore, all policies and practices adopted to prevent terrorism must be firmly grounded in respect for human rights and the rule of law. Second, it is vital to take a comprehensive approach to terrorism which encompasses not only essential security-based counter-terrorism measures, but also systematic preventative measures which address the root causes of violent extremism. These include lack of socio-economic opportunities; marginalization and discrimination; poor governance; violations of human rights and the rule of law; prolonged and unresolved conflicts; and radicalization in prisons. The creation of open, equitable, inclusive, and pluralist societies, based on the full respect of human rights and with economic opportunities for all, represents the most tangible and meaningful alternative to violent extremism and the most promising strategy for undermining its appeal.[3]

---

3   Plan of Action to Prevent Violent Extremism, Report of the Secretary General, A/70/674 (available at http://www.un.org/en/ga/search/view_doc.asp?symbol= A/70/674).

4. Social and Economic Rights

In addition to civil and political rights, the UDHR contains a list of social and economic rights. These are set out in Articles 22 to 26, which include provisions relating to social security, conditions of work, rest and leisure, standard of living, and education.

The inclusion of these rights occasioned some concern in the decades following the adoption of the UDHR and their inclusion continues to be controversial for some who resist the idea that these rights are as central as civil and political rights. Others argue that they are *more* central. And some think of them as social and economic aspirations but doubt whether the language of rights makes sense.

Much of the success of the human rights movement over nearly seven decades is attributable to the creation of a set of standards that can be upheld without changing the structures of international affairs and the international economy. While social and economic rights were included in the UDHR, they differ from this paradigm in that their realization might be thought to require some restructuring of the international order. This challenges us to consider the extent to which social and economic objectives should be pursued through a human rights framework.

4.1 The importance of social and economic rights

The Commission believes that social and economic rights are vital. They reflect genuine human needs that every state has an obligation to attend to, within existing resources, in the interest of all those committed to their care.

    http://dx.doi.org/10.11647/OBP.0091.09

Social and economic rights are conceptually linked to civil and political rights because respect for human dignity requires that both be upheld. There is also a causal connection in that civil and political rights can be used to secure social and economic rights, and social and economic rights make possible the meaningful exercise of civil and political rights. Indeed, the failure of social and economic rights makes individuals more vulnerable to other human rights abuses, such as forced labor. Dire poverty and the other ills and vulnerabilities that come with it are a standard threat to rights of all kinds. So we think it is fitting and valuable to have social and economic rights enshrined in the same declaration as civil and political rights, and thus to perceive human rights as a whole in the context of a single declaration.

It is right for the world to indicate to governments that attention to matters of social security, conditions of work, rest and leisure, standard of living, health, and education are now regarded as elementary and fundamental tasks of government, laid down as compelling priorities in relation to whatever resources are available. The rights here are not optional and they are not just wistful longings. A lack of resources does not turn such rights into a mere wish list. Countries have a categorical obligation to do all that they reasonably can to fulfil these rights. Moreover, other states and all international organizations have an obligation to assist particular countries in this regard.

We add two further points. First, the social and economic part of the UDHR is not intended as a comprehensive theory of good government, nor is it intended as a theory of social justice. It is supposed to capture no more than the essence of certain elementary obligations that societies owe to their members in the social and economic sphere. Second, the Declaration does not commit societies to economic equality, but requires that specified areas of concern be attended to. In wealthier nations, much more generous provisions can and should be made for health, education, and social security than in developing nations. Nevertheless, the mandate is that every society, within its resources, should pay due attention to the health, education, and social security of its members.

The value and relevance of Articles 22 to 26 are not just in the immediate requirements they impose. Like other articles of the UDHR, these provisions lay down a foundation for a subsequent and wider comprehension of human rights. In the case of social and economic rights, the articles of the UDHR prefigured and prepared the way for the ICESCR; the development of international agencies devoted to securing these rights, directly and indirectly; the inclusion of social and economic rights in modern national constitutions (and their elaboration by courts in the context of national constitutional law); and the evolution of doctrines for benchmarks and core provision of these rights.

4.2 Relation to availability of resources

Social and economic rights are dependent on the availability and distribution of resources in a way that civil and political rights are not. It is true that civil and political rights do have their costs and, in some circumstances, social and economic rights require forbearance rather than costly action. But in general, the level of provision needed for social and economic rights is high. So paying attention to the capacity of the actors responsible for delivering these rights is both natural and unavoidable. It is a matter of debate – among all commentators on the UDHR – whether Articles 22 to 26 should be read as stipulating a common core of minimum provision or whether the provision that is expected should vary with the social and economic circumstances and expectations of each society.

One view is that it would be dangerous to attempt to stipulate a common core of provision at some fixed level. First, the standards might be so minimal that while some countries would deem it an achievement to meet them, a number of other countries would lose ground. Second, if certain developing countries knew that they were unable to meet the minimum standards, they would be less likely to ratify human rights instruments.

However, the more persuasive view is that we should be uncompromising on social and economic rights as they are formulated, but recognize some degree of relativity in capacities and context. Specifically, we should keep faith with the Declaration's explicit universality, both as to actual provision and as to the expectations that people are entitled to. The social and economic provisions of the UDHR should be interpreted to mean that everyone is entitled to certain minimum standards of health, education, and social security. The concept of dignity – while abstract – provides a yardstick against which to set minimum measures. The extent of available resources is one determinative factor, though the UDHR also imposes constraints on the allocation of such resources as there are: the UDHR mandates that the actors responsible for social and economic rights give priority to health, education, and social security based on resources that can reasonably be made available given economic and fiscal circumstances, rather than on the resources that actually are made available. It is possible that these rights may permit a reasonable level of cultural relativity: to take Article 23, what counts as "an existence worthy of human dignity" may vary from one set of social and cultural circumstances to another. However, the Commission does not accept the idea that there are cultural differences that can affect who should benefit from social and economic rights or can justify maldistribution in this regard. So, for example, we do not believe that people should ever be denied equal social and economic rights because they are women or ethnic minorities.

While we must face up to the task of setting reasonably clear common standards for minimum provision, it is equally imperative to acknowledge the phenomenon of extreme poverty, where there is no question that people are living well below the most minimum levels that human dignity would demand. In short, we will often be in a position to conclude that there has been a violation of social and economic rights, without having to specify a standard at the upper level.

The Commission believes that the UDHR (and the ICESCR) should be read as endorsing an ongoing global conversation about what the minimum provision should be and a rule of progress to the effect that the human rights framework calls for steps to improve the position of everyone, including the least advantaged in society.

4.3 Responsibilities for social and economic rights

To a certain extent, a poor state can act on the internal distribution of its resources but it cannot directly act to secure an equitable global distribution of resources that would enable it to end the poverty of its citizens. Social and economic rights therefore raise questions about the allocation of responsibilities, and particularly whether and to what extent wealthy states have an obligation to help citizens of poor states.

It is arguable that we should be sensitive to the relationship between the responsibilities that certain rights impose and the capacities that the responsible actors have to fulfill them, a balance which is particularly relevant in the context of social and economic rights. Certainly, it might be thought that any adequate approach to human rights needs to take a realistic view of the capacities of the responsible actors, and of the resources they can control and dispense. A realistic view of the actual powers and resources of state and non-state agents must take proper account of the effects of globalization and the ways in which power has been reconfigured. At the same time, lack of resources does not entitle any government to ignore its own obligations. The social and economic rights set out in the UDHR require governments to do everything reasonable within their power to implement these provisions, including redressing priorities in the allocation of resources.

This raises a broader point: is it true that you can only articulate rights after you have identified the responsible authority – a duty-bearer – and determined that their violation is actionable? The Commission's conclusion is that we are often in a position to identify a right before we are in a position to identify the duty-bearers charged with fulfilling that right. Each right gives us a reason to seek duty-bearers, but where we look will depend on the circumstances. And there may be many duties and many duty-bearers corresponding to a given right. Thus we should think of duty-bearers of social and economic rights – and indeed rights generally – as standing not in a static but in a dynamic relation to a given right. This accords with the way philosophers analyze the relation between rights and duties.

We have to recognize that we are not always dealing with straightforward, concrete rights violations, but instead with a plethora of ways in which there can be failures of responsibility. There are those who are able to act to bring about progress on social and economic rights, but who may not have full agency with regard to a violation *per se.* Responsibilities will therefore be both direct and indirect. More broadly, systems that sustain long-term global poverty are matters of deep concern, and the international community must question arrangements that do not further the attainment of social and economic rights. This puts the issue of poverty onto the agenda for citizens, states, corporations, and international institutions – which is one of the most powerful ways in which social and economic rights operate.

The Commission believes that states have front-line responsibility for the social and economic well-being of their citizens. Fair economic growth has a critical role to play in this, and the Commission believes it is crucial to see a stronger connection between economic policy and the instruments of human rights. The support of the international community should to some extent be conditioned on whether the governments of particular countries are discharging their own responsibilities. The UDHR leaves open the question of placing social and economic rights in a constitution and the question of their justiciability in the courts. We judge that the most likely vehicle for implementation of these rights is social legislation rather than the constitution of each country. And another issue – an open one – is whether it is wise to allocate enforcement here to courts.

It is evident, however, that the challenges faced by many states cannot be resolved entirely by actions in those states alone. The Commission believes that there is an overwhelming moral case for interpreting the social and economic rights provisions of the Declaration as placing obligations on the international community to alleviate world poverty. International aid and transfers, aimed at strengthening the capacity of recipient states to secure the social and economic rights of their citizens, thus have an indispensable role to play.

Three more specific points are worth mentioning. First, it is clear that many low-income and middle-income countries cannot afford to tackle the poverty of their citizens entirely by themselves. Analysis by the World Bank shows that even if those countries were to tax their middle class to the limit, it would not generate enough resources to eradicate their endemic poverty.[1] Second, there are approximately 700 million people in the world who currently live on less than 1.90 USD a day. However, the amount of money needed to bring these people out of such extreme poverty is small in relation to the world's resources. Third, in 1970, the UN General Assembly agreed that all "economically advanced countries" should dedicate 0.7 percent of their gross national

---

1   http://blogs.worldbank.org/developmenttalk/should-we-care-equally-about-poor-people-wherever-they-may-live

income to official development assistance. Nonetheless, in 2013 only Denmark, Luxembourg, Norway, Sweden, the United Arab Emirates, and the United Kingdom spent more than 0.7 percent on aid. Social and economic rights are an international and not just a national responsibility.

Responsibilities among the international community to uphold social and economic rights are in the Commission's view held not only by states, but also above the level of states by international organizations and below the level of states by corporations and individuals. Issues of world poverty cannot be dealt with exclusively by nations or by a transfer of resources between nations. Global businesses have a substantial and at times decisive impact on the social and economic rights of millions of people worldwide. Their role can be positive or negative. Over the last third of a century, the expansion of the global economy, led by the private sector, has been the driving force in lifting almost two billion people out of extreme poverty. But in too many instances businesses have also frustrated government efforts to protect the social and economic welfare of their people, and have been implicated in violations of social and economic rights. Redefining the legal obligations of corporations is of course a difficult and complicated matter. There is, however, an emerging demand for companies to recognize and act on responsibilities arising out of human rights in their global operations, including the right to just conditions of work. Drawing on the inspiration of the UDHR, companies and other stakeholders are beginning to shape industry-specific human rights standards and metrics.

4.4 Poverty reduction and other human rights

It is sometimes said that, although the rights in the Declaration are presented as an interconnected body of principles, complementary and mutually supportive, there are in fact serious conflicts among them. It is sometimes argued, for example, that the right to freedom of speech or assembly may conflict with the right of people not to live in poverty, that the only way to lift large numbers of people out of poverty may involve authoritarian rule. Or, to take another example, it is sometimes argued that the right to life and security may conflict with the right to privacy, that ensuring that innocent civilians are not subject to violent attacks may involve curbing their rights not to be surveilled.

It is important to appreciate that, to the extent to which there is a "trade-off" among various rights, it is not a conflict among the rights *themselves*. The principles of the UDHR are entirely consistent with one another and may all derive from a single foundation.

What *is* true is that, in certain very specific real-world settings, our ability to *fully implement* one right may conflict with our ability to *fully implement* another, at least temporarily. This is not a logical conflict among the rights themselves, but rather a reflection of the way in which real-world conditions can put pressure on the simultaneous implementation of several rights.

However, no claim that there exists, in a specific real-world setting, a tension between the implementation of one right and that of another is ever self-evident. Any such claim would be very hard to establish and must always be subjected to the most rigorous scrutiny.

Furthermore, it is always a serious question whether any particular proposed trade-off is morally justifiable. Even if it were true that, under the pressure of certain sorts of threat, a greater emphasis on preserving the right to life might require curbing the right to privacy, it is not obvious what this should entail. We must be able to choose whether we prefer to live in a surveillance society or whether we prefer to live in a freer society that runs a somewhat greater risk of unpredictable attacks on its citizens.

The implementation of human rights is a historical process, in which fulfillment is often and in varying degrees incomplete and uneven. It is a complex process too, involving not just the avoidance of violations but the setting up and maintaining of social, political, and legal systems and institutions. This is necessarily a protracted and asymmetrical process. So, in all of this, progress, not perfection, should be the measure.

5. Responsibility for Human Rights

These issues of social and economic rights have put the subject of responsibility firmly on the table, but we thought it appropriate to address it at a more general level as well.

Responsibility for rights has a number of aspects. In this section we are concerned with two of them: first, responsibilities for securing the subject matter of each right; and second, responsibilities of rights-bearers themselves. A third set of responsibilities – for monitoring, investigating, and remedying rights violations – is discussed in section 6.

The UDHR enumerates rights, but it does not specify who carries the corresponding duties. The Declaration seems to assume that states are the primary bearers of responsibility. There is also a suggestion in the document that responsibility for upholding human rights may fall on individuals and entities below the level of the state, and on organizations above the level of the state. Indeed, the proclamation clause of the preamble states that "every individual and every organ of society, keeping this Declaration constantly in mind, shall strive by teaching and education to promote respect for these rights and freedoms and by progressive measures, national and international, to secure their universal and effective recognition and observance." Moreover, Article 28 provides that "everyone is entitled to a social and international order in which the rights and freedoms set forth in this Declaration can be fully realized."

     http://dx.doi.org/10.11647/OBP.0091.10

For some rights – such as the due process provisions in Articles 9 to 11 – it is obvious that states are the principal targets of the constraints. For the rest, the explanation for the UDHR's openness on the question of responsibilities probably has more to do with the political resistance that would have met any attempt at explicit specification in 1947 and 1948. This would have been especially true of any attempt to specify international or nation-to-nation obligations in regard to social and economic rights. It might also have been true of social and economic rights generally, inasmuch as debate about the specification of duty-bearers would have opened up intense ideological disagreement about political economy.

While acknowledging the obstacles that would have faced any effort at specification in 1948, our task now is to expand on the reference to "every individual and every organ of society" in the preamble and on the reference to everyone as "entitled to a social and international order in which the rights and freedoms set forth in this Declaration can be fully realized" in Article 28. The rights in the Declaration should be understood as generating duties for states, international institutions, corporations, private persons, and even rights-bearing individuals themselves.

5.1 The special role of states

The role of states remains essential. Given the realities of our world – this was even more the case in 1948 – states must be regarded as the main guarantors of the rights of their own citizens. States still control the basic structure of each nation's polity and legal system, and the overall structure of governance in each society. This is true whether we are talking about civil and political rights or social and economic rights.

States are duty-bound to the human rights of their citizens in several ways. First, states have inherent responsibility for certain institutions, like the legal system, which human rights directly constrain. Second, states also have a degree of control over other institutions and structures on which human rights impose limitations. Third, states have a greater power of enforcement against rights-violators than any other entity in society. Fourth, and conversely, states can become a major threat to human rights. Fifth, and fortunately, states also can furnish – through the division of their powers – the major safeguard against state-based threats.

The special position of states is not just a matter of effectiveness and control. States claim a form of legitimacy that distinguishes them from other entities and agencies operating, whether lawfully or unlawfully, in a society. The UDHR and the covenants aim to impose human rights-based conditions on this legitimacy.

The laws and national constitutions of states, in most instances, will be the first recourse to address any violations of human rights, and should be regarded as the ordinary mode of human rights implementation. Indeed, the human rights regime initiated by the UDHR was intended as a foundation not only for the subsequent covenants and international agreements, but also for the laws and national constitutions of individual countries.

In a globalized world, it is also the duty of each state to concern itself to a certain extent with the human rights of persons outside its borders, taking into account the following four forms of influence: first, the effect of the state's own policies and actions on other countries; second, the impact on other countries of the way in which it participates in international institutions; third, the provision and efficacy of development aid; and fourth, the response to rights abuses in other countries, either by way of criticism and public denunciation or, in the last resort, by intervention and support for intervention.

While states have the primary responsibility for ensuring the human rights of their citizens, there are numerous examples of situations where governments no longer control substantial tracts of territory, no longer control the military or have a monopoly on force, lack legitimacy, and are unable or unwilling to provide public services. In these situations, who is responsible for the human rights of the population? This issue needs to be urgently addressed by the international community.

5.2 Other entities

The fact that one entity – like a state – has responsibility for a given right is quite compatible with other entities also having their own obligations. Rights generate waves of responsibility, and those responsibilities may fall on an array of duty-bearers.

a. Sub-national governments

Though national state responsibility is primary, the position of sub-national governments also needs to be addressed. Often the governments of local, devolved, provincial, and state entities have considerable autonomy, and they may not be entirely under the control of the national government so far as upholding rights is concerned.

b. International institutions

Global and regional institutions, including those associated with the UN (like the Security Council), the IMF, and the World Bank, should regard themselves as bound by human rights. Even if they do not have an affirmative responsibility to provide what is necessary for rights, they have a responsibility not to undermine human rights or make them more difficult to secure. Even when an organization believes itself to have a legal immunity, it is appropriate for that immunity to be waived in cases of egregious violations of human rights. The Commission believes that these responsibilities should be made explicit. The Commission also calls for international institutions to sign and ratify international human rights agreements.

c. Corporations

Since 1948, the power concentrated in global companies has reached unprecedented levels. When country gross domestic product (**GDP**) is compared to annual company revenues, half of the 100 largest economies in the world today are private corporations. States have a responsibility to exercise appropriate oversight over corporations operating in their jurisdictions, to ensure their compliance with human rights standards. In practice, however, many states have been unable or unwilling to act. Companies often operate in weak states where there is a profound governance gap. They have also flexed their political and economic influence to undermine state oversight, by demanding deregulation and by lobbying for business-friendly regulations that diminish the capacity of governments to promote environmental and social protection.

In light of this expansion in corporate power and the governance gap in many states, there should be a firm expectation that companies will respect human rights. Stakeholders, shareholders, employees, and constituencies including civil society, responsible investors, trade unions, and consumers are increasingly demanding that corporations attend seriously to policies and practices addressing human rights. Generational shifts in attitudes to consumption and broader access to information on company operations through new media sources are also exerting pressure on companies to comply with the human rights standards applicable to their industries. In 2011, the UN adopted the Guiding Principles on Business and Human Rights, which establishes a "protect, respect and remedy framework" that requires businesses to adhere to policies and practices that respect human rights in their day-to-day business operations. Over time, companies have also agreed to be bound by various international obligations, for example through their participation in the framework of the International Labour Organization (**ILO**), which is committed to dialogue and cooperation among governments, employers, and workers, and to the development of standards addressing conditions of work.

Given that the bulk of the world's employment is in the private sector, the Commission considers that certain provisions of the UDHR, such as Article 23 on the conditions of work, should be interpreted as imposing duties on corporations. Of course, national governments have the primary responsibility for establishing and enforcing the legal frameworks within which businesses operate. But in the many situations where national governments are failing to protect their own people, it is incumbent on global corporations and their investors and financiers to develop and abide by human rights standards that extend beyond the jurisdiction of any one state.

We must also accept that the role and importance of business organizations reaches beyond conditions of work. Corporations have become important actors alongside states, and perform governance functions that transcend their roles as employers and workplace proprietors. They also play a prominent part in the communities in which they operate, and have a major impact on issues of migration, food security, the empowerment of women, and environmental sustainability. Consequently, companies have obligations in these areas, not only to respect but also to advance human rights in the states where they do business.

There are reasons to believe that the influence of large global companies will continue to multiply. This points to the need for new mechanisms to strengthen corporate compliance with human rights. Engaged citizens, stakeholders, and civil society groups have an indispensable role to play in working with corporations to develop practical and effective ways to secure human rights. Such efforts should be undertaken in collaboration with national governments, taking into account the willingness and capacity of states to protect their own people. When states fail to act, corporations and other stakeholders need to develop alternative measures to ensure that basic rights are being respected.

Thus companies need to work with key stakeholders to develop industry minimum standards on human rights, and metrics to monitor and assess compliance. Multi-stakeholder initiatives that hold businesses accountable to agreed standards through reporting and monitoring can help drive a race to the top and give consumers and investors the information they need and are now demanding to guide their purchasing and investment decisions.

Home states, which directly benefit from the economic activity generated by global companies, must take steps to ensure that companies under their jurisdiction respect human rights in their operations abroad.

d. Private persons

The Commission is attracted to the idea that individuals – ordinary men and women – should be thought of as the ultimate bearers of the duties that correspond to human rights. In the final analysis it is everyone's responsibility to respect and look out for each other's rights. (This does not replace the primary responsibility of states, since states are the main mechanism through which people carry out their duties in regard to human rights and the mechanism by which their duties are coordinated and made effective.)

With respect to rights that rely on fiscal resources – social and economic rights in particular – individuals have clear duties as taxpayers. More generally, citizens have negative duties not to oppose or agitate against human rights. They may also have positive duties to form social movements and NGOs that actively support and lobby for human rights. They have duties to play their part in maintaining a culture of rights in society and in the world at large. And individuals have the responsibilities of global citizenship in relation to the specific demands of human rights.

Article 29(1) of the UDHR is germane in this context. It asserts that "everyone has duties to the community in which alone the free and full development of his personality is possible." From the perspective of global citizenship, "community" means not just the national community but also the world community, whose structures increasingly protect or deny human rights at every level: local, national, and global.

5.3 Responsibilities of rights-bearers

Finally, we emphasize again that rights-bearers themselves have responsibilities with respect to their own rights and responsibilities as rights-bearers to the rights system as a whole and to society generally.

The responsibility of rights-bearers requires us to recognize that: rights may at times be legitimately limited; there is a duty to listen to and consider any reasons given for the limitation of rights; and that the fulfilment of some rights is costly and that this may render rights not immediately achievable. In a sense, these responsibilities recognize the need for us to have a democratic dialogue about the fulfilment of rights, and a dialogue requires a commitment to both listening and engaging. We believe that if the value of dialogue on rights is recognized, the protection and fulfilment of human rights is likely to be advanced.

Some commentators argue that rights-bearers often act irresponsibly in claiming human rights protections by being over-zealous in pursuing rights campaigns or by adopting the posture of victim. In our view, such commentary risks downplaying or soft-pedalling human rights abuses or blocking serious and important interpretive debates. Human rights are designed, among other things, to protect people from the worst evils that can be inflicted on them. They are designed to facilitate a clamoring for attention for victims of abuse, even when this is uncomfortable for other members of society. We must never lose sight of this.

Sometimes the complaint is that rights are being claimed by individuals who have already shown that they are socially irresponsible or who are accused of crimes or suspected of terrorism. We believe that not the slightest concession should be made to this critique of human rights. Just as Articles 18 and 19 of the UDHR are intended, among other purposes, to protect those who hold dissident views or who believe in an unpopular creed, so certain human rights must be understood as operating for the benefit of those who have come under public suspicion of crime or other anti-social activity. We view with horror the suggestion that these protections should be diminished on the grounds of "responsibility."

Of course, a culture of human rights should not foster a purely passive sense of entitlement. This may be even truer when we think about social and economic rights that specify and privilege certain material interests that all people have – interests in social security, in an income sufficient for "an existence worthy of human dignity," in rest and leisure, in a certain standard of living and of health, and so on. That these rights are expressed as such in a document that – whatever else it does – imposes duties upon states should not be read as meaning that the state has the sole responsibility here. Instead, and this must be acknowledged and emphasized, the UDHR assumes that primary provision for most of these rights will be made by individuals themselves through gainful work and employment. That is the heart of Article 23. It affirms that, wherever possible, individuals have a duty to provide for themselves and for those who are dependent upon them. And in recognizing that the economy must be such as to satisfy certain conditions – adequate remuneration, justice in the conditions of work, worker organization, and holidays with pay, amongst others – the UDHR by no means retreats from the position that in this context individuals too are responsible for themselves.

Nor is any such retreat envisioned in the Declaration's call to make provision, socially and collectively if necessary, for the well-being of the most vulnerable. Again, that does not detract from the central principle in these articles that individuals, broadly speaking, have a responsibility as well as a right to work for a living. The Commission is adamantly opposed to any critique of social and economic rights that ignores this or that contends or implies that social and economic rights foster a culture of idle entitlement.

5.4 No closed model of responsibility

It would be a mistake to develop a rigid or closed model of responsibility for rights, or to conclude that rights are of no value until responsibilities are actually specified. The advantage of specifying rights first is that this provides a basis for thinking about the duties of the state and other entities.

The Commission has judged that it is both sensible and essential to retain an open and developing sense of where responsibilities lie, since the environment in which rights have to be satisfied is constantly changing.

6. Implementation of Human Rights

6.1 Introduction

The framers of the UDHR, led by Eleanor Roosevelt, envisaged three parts to the postwar human rights enterprise: a set of general principles; the codification of those principles into law; and practical means of implementation.[1]

Today implementation takes many forms, ranging from top-down monitoring by human rights treaty bodies and adjudication by international courts and tribunals, to capacity building in civil society organizations and human rights education at the grass-roots level. We should recognize that effective implementation includes not only retrospective complaint mechanisms, but also forward-looking efforts to cultivate respect for human rights. This is reflected in the mandate of the Office of the High Commissioner for Human Rights, which is both to promote and protect human rights.

---

1   Mary Ann Glendon, *A World Made New: Eleanor Roosevelt and the Universal Declaration of Human Rights* (London: Random House, 2001), Chapter 6. At its second meeting – in Geneva in December 1947 – the Human Rights Commission pressed forward in three working groups. The first group, chaired by Eleanor Roosevelt, worked on the draft Declaration. The second group, chaired by Lord Dukeston of the United Kingdom, sought to prepare a draft Convention. The third group, chaired by Hansa Mehta of India, investigated methods of implementation that might or might not later be incorporated into a Covenant.

        http://dx.doi.org/10.11647/OBP.0091.11

The Commission's starting point in considering human rights implementation is Article 28 of the UDHR, which provides that "everyone is entitled to a social and international order in which the rights and freedoms set forth in this Declaration can be fully realized." This statement invites us to focus on the disparity between the world as it is, and the world we should hope to live in. More specifically, it raises the question of why the human rights embedded in the UDHR are far from realized today, and what more the international community can – and must – do to make real the ideal of human rights for all. This section of the report deals with that challenge.

In sections 6.2 and 6.3, we look at particular areas of rights, to give an indication of how the implementation of human rights is faring, and we develop a number of specific suggestions. In 6.4, we take on some more general issues about sovereignty and state responsibility, identifying the obstacles to and the opportunities for the greater vindication of human rights.

6.2 State of play on representative rights

The Commission has considered the implementation of the following representative provisions of the UDHR: the anti-slavery provision (Article 4); the anti-torture provision (Article 5); the free expression provision (Article 19) and the free association provision (Article 20); and the education provision (Article 26). We singled out these articles because they represent some of the most pressing human rights concerns of the early twenty-first century.

We set out below short summaries of the Commission's conclusions with respect to each of these rights. The full case studies, on which these findings are based, are set out in Online Appendix E.[2]

---

2   Appendix E, on Human Rights Implementation, is available at https://www.openbookpublishers.com/isbn/9781783742189#resources. The case studies on the anti-slavery provision, the anti-torture provision, the free expression and free association provisions, and the education provision were prepared for the Commission by the Center on Global Justice (University of California, San Diego). The case study on the equality and non-discrimination provision – which the Commission also considered in its analysis of human rights implementation – was prepared by Dr. Dimitrina Petrova, the founding Executive Director of the Equal Rights Trust.

a. Anti-slavery (Article 4)

Slavery constitutes a profound human rights violation and an affront to any sense of human dignity. While definitions vary, at its core slavery involves one person taking away another person's freedom – their freedom to leave their workplace or employer/slavemaster at their own choosing, to control their body, to choose their work – so that they can be exploited. This is achieved not through lawful means (as is the case with military service or imprisonment) but through threats, violence, or coercion.

The concept of slavery and slavery-like practices can cover a range of practices, including forced labor (e.g., debt bondage, serfdom, and forced sex work), exploitative child labor (e.g., child soldiers), descent-based slavery, forced or servile marriage (e.g., exchanging a woman for payment), and human trafficking. They all have in common an inability for the individual to leave a workplace or employer/slavemaster at their own free will.

Article 4 of the UDHR asserts that "No one shall be held in slavery or servitude; slavery and the slave trade shall be prohibited in all their forms." This prohibition has been reaffirmed in a range of treaty provisions: Article 8 of the ICCPR, Article 5 of the African Charter on Human and Peoples' Rights, Article 6 of the American Convention on Human Rights, Article 10 of the Arab Charter on Human Rights, Article 13 of the Association of Southeast Asian Nations Human Rights Declaration, and Article 4 of the European Convention on Human Rights. The Rome Statute of the International Criminal Court criminalizes, as crimes against humanity, enslavement, sexual slavery, and enforced prostitution. As war crimes, it criminalizes sexual slavery and enforced prostitution. In addition, there are a number of conventions that aim to eradicate slavery, most notably the 1926 Slavery Convention, as amended by the 1956 Supplementary Convention on the Abolition of Slavery; the 2000 International Labour Organization Convention Concerning the Prohibition and Immediate Action for the Elimination of the Worst Forms of Child Labour; and the 2000 Protocol to Prevent, Suppress and Punish Trafficking in Persons, Especially Women and Children. In 2007, the Human Rights Council established a Special Rapporteur on contemporary forms of slavery, including its causes and consequences.

Despite this extensive array of treaty provisions embodying the spirit of Article 4 of the UDHR, slavery persists across the world, even in countries that have ratified anti-slavery treaties. According to ILO estimates, almost 21 million individuals across the globe were forced laborers in 2012; 11.4 million of them were female and 9.5 million were male. Walk Free estimates of modern slavery – which include forced marriage – place the number of people living in servitude far higher at 35.8 million. Children are particularly vulnerable, especially as child soldiers, domestic servants, and sex slaves. Against this reality, the U.S. Department of State estimates that there are only around 10,000 prosecutions annually for human trafficking offences.

Clearly, the task of preventing slavery is not as straightforward as simply declaring it to be illegal. Slavery has different root causes, and many factors that sustain both vulnerability to enslavement and the impunity of offenders. Conflict, corruption, poverty, and discrimination are key drivers of vulnerability, as are historical relationships of power, colonialism, and exploitation – relationships that have become embedded in local culture and social norms. Weak rule of law, the failure of legal systems to operate effectively across international borders, failure of social safety nets, and even the normalization of some forms of exploitation facilitate the continued existence of slavery.

Ending slavery is deeply connected with the mission of the UDHR. This will require a deep focus on discrimination and inequality, and the systems that allow these to persist. It will require governments, corporations, and private citizens to focus serious attention (and resources) on practical realization of the social and economic rights that allow people to protect themselves from slavery, whether this is through social insurance in times of shocks, food and shelter in times of crisis, or their ability to access decent work. It will require governments to address the corruption that perpetuates the impunity of offenders.

b. Anti-torture (Article 5)

Torture has enduring effects on the physical, mental, and emotional well-being of its survivors, crippling or destroying their abilities to pursue fulfillment and happiness. In many nations, torture is used to extract confessions from alleged criminals or political prisoners. Torture is utterly inconsistent with basic human rights.

Article 5 of the UDHR states: "No one shall be subjected to torture or to cruel, inhuman, or degrading treatment or punishment." Since torture has devastating consequences for its victims, the international prohibition against it is absolute. Article 7 of the ICCPR reaffirms the UDHR's proscription of torture, and expressly bans non-consensual medical or scientific experimentation. Most importantly, the United Nations Convention Against Torture and Other Cruel, Inhuman or Degrading Treatment or Punishment obliges every country to take effective legislative, administrative, and judicial measures to prevent torture in any territory under its jurisdiction (Article 2.1), and forbids states from sending a person to another state where they would be in danger of being tortured (Article 3). The 158 state parties to CAT are required to ban the use of evidence obtained through torture in their courts (Article 15). In addition, CAT provides that all state parties must ensure "education and information regarding the prohibition against torture are fully included in the training of law enforcement personnel," or any other persons who are involved in interrogations of those arrested, detained, or imprisoned (Article 10.1).

The repudiation of torture is supposed to be realized in international law through three primary mechanisms. First, CAT establishes a Committee against Torture that reviews reports submitted by state parties on the measures they have taken to fulfill their obligations under the convention. The Committee also initiates inquiries concerning allegations of systematic torture by a state party. Second, the Optional Protocol to CAT (*OPCAT*) establishes an international inspection system for places of detention with the objective of preventing torture, modeled on the system that has existed in Europe since 1987 (the Committee for the Prevention of Torture). Third, in 1985 the UN Commission on Human Rights established the Special Rapporteur on torture and other cruel, inhuman, or degrading treatment or punishment. The Special Rapporteur examines relevant questions in all countries, regardless of whether a state has ratified CAT or OPCAT.

Nevertheless, torture remains a shamefully common practice. Amnesty International reported that torture occurred in 144 countries – scattered across all continents – between January 2009 and May 2013. Torture takes many forms. In 2013 to 2014 alone, Amnesty International documented over 27 variants worldwide, the most common of which were beatings, electric shocks, stress positions, extended isolation, and whipping.

Why is torture so persistent and pervasive? First, many countries have not adopted domestic laws criminalizing it. Second, even where there are laws against torture, real steps to bar it are often not taken. Third, victims frequently come from the ranks of the marginal and the vulnerable such as minority groups, the poor, and opposition political parties and movements. They have little or no power to demand and obtain redress. Fourth, international efforts to combat torture are limited by a lack of data identifying where violations occur most and who suffers them most. Finally, anti-torture efforts are undermined by the widespread misconception that torture is an efficient and reliable shortcut to establish guilt and secure justice. A survey conducted in 2013–2014 by Amnesty International across 21 countries and 21,000 respondents found that over a third of them agreed that torture is sometimes "necessary and acceptable."

c. Free expression (Article 19) and free association (Article 20)

Although enumerated in separate articles of the UDHR (Articles 19 and 20), freedom of opinion, expression, assembly, and association (collectively, *expression rights*) are inextricably linked. Expression rights are both essential for good government and central to the affirmation of the dignity of every individual. They are accordingly the hallmark of a free and open society.

Article 19 affirms: "Everyone has the right to freedom of opinion and expression; this right includes freedom to hold opinions without interference and to seek, receive and impart information and ideas through any media and regardless of frontiers." Article 20 is similarly emphatic: "(1) Everyone has the right to freedom of peaceful assembly and association," and "(2) No one may be compelled to belong to an association."

Articles 19, 21, and 22 of the ICCPR collectively declare wide-ranging rights in the domains of opinion, expression, assembly, and association. Article 19 guarantees the right to "hold opinions without interference," as well as the ability to "seek and impart information and ideas of all kinds [...] through any other media regardless of frontiers." Article 21 upholds the right to peaceful assembly, while Article 22 insists on the right to free association, including, notably, "the right to form and join trade unions." Article 8 of the ICESCR extends the right to trade unions to national and international confederations, and clearly enshrines the right to strike as a bargaining tool. The ICCPR and ICESCR establish a set of exceptions to expression, assembly, and association rights, for the protection of national security, public order and safety, and public health and morals.

A number of other international treaties have widened the writ of the ICCPR and the ICESCR, setting out distinct prohibitions against specific types of dissent-suppression. Most prominently, the Convention for the Elimination of all Forms of Discrimination Against Women and the Convention on the Rights of the Child explicitly declare that expression rights are women's rights and children's rights too. Regional treaties – including the European Convention on Human Rights, the American Convention on Human Rights, the African Charter on Human and People's Rights, and the ASEAN Human Rights Declaration – have likewise broadened the recognition of expression rights in the post-war period. Generally, regional treaties have followed the template of the ICCPR, protecting conscience, expression, association, and assembly – with exceptions for public health and morals, national security, public order, and harm to others' rights and reputations.

Although there has been a degree of progress in securing expression rights, they are not observed today in many parts of the world. The Commission notes that three actors bear particular responsibility for advancing expression rights: states, international organizations, and corporations.

States are obviously of key importance here. Although many national constitutions affirm rights to freedom of opinion, expression, assembly, and association, they are impermissibly circumscribed by states. Restrictions on expression rights must be proportionate, necessary, and lawful in order to be justified. However, many countries routinely suppress expression, particularly political dissent. State interference in four areas is of pressing concern: first, Internet censorship and surveillance; second, the blocking of funds to civil society organizations (*CSOs*); third, burdensome restraints on assembly; and fourth, the detention of and violence directed at journalists.

International organizations must also defend and extend expression rights. Currently a number of international organizations erect barriers to CSO participation and engagement with their work. They should reduce barriers to participation in their decision-making and foster active stakeholder engagement. Corporations too have an obligation to observe expression rights, including the right to unionize and to protest near places of business.

d. Education (Article 26)

The right to education is both a human right in itself and an indispensable means of realizing other human rights. Education empowers individuals to raise themselves out of poverty and advance their socio-economic status. Politically and socially, education offers people the necessary skills to identify common goals, assume a full and active place in community life, recognize manipulative media practices, and resist oppression. Despite its vital importance in securing human rights and advancing socio-economic development, education commands too little media attention. There is a stubborn and unacceptable gap between education needs and available resources. Indeed, total global financial support for education has actually *fallen* in recent years.

The right to education is articulated in Article 26 of the UDHR, which emphasizes universality, equal access, and the role of education in promoting respect for human rights and tolerance among nations and social groups. The right to education is likewise reaffirmed in Article 13 of the ICESCR and Articles 28 and 29 of the CRC. The major regional human rights instruments similarly recognize a universal right to education, including the African Charter on Human and Peoples' Rights (Article 17(1)), the European Convention on Human Rights (Article 2 of the First Protocol), and the Association of Southeast Asian Nations' Human Rights Declaration (Article 31). One exception is the American Convention on Human Rights, which lacks a specific provision on education. The Commission on Human Rights appointed a Special Rapporteur on Education in 1998. In 2000, the Special Rapporteur developed the Right to Education Project, supported by prominent international NGOs, including ActionAid International, Amnesty International, Save the Children, and Human Rights Watch. Again and again the international community has set higher goals for progress in education. Quantitative targets have been set in the Millennium Development Goals (*MDGs*), the Education for All (*EFA*) movement, and the SDGs.

Unfortunately, although gains were made on these goals in the early 2000s – reducing the number of out of school children from 120 million to less than 60 million – further progress has stalled. For example, in recent years, the number of out of school children has *increased* from 58 to 59 million. In order to reverse this trend, the 4-A framework for education must be fulfilled. The 4-A framework emphasizes **availability** of educational institutions and programs, the physical and economic **accessibility** of educational institutions and programs to everyone without discrimination, the **acceptability** of curricula and teaching methods (e.g., culturally appropriate and good quality), and the **adaptability** of education to diverse social and cultural settings, as well as to students' special requirements.

There are four primary barriers to achieving the right to education: first, lack of investment and finance; second, economic barriers to access for both children and adults; third, discrimination, particularly gender-based discrimination; and fourth, challenges in large-scale emergency situations. According to a 2015 UNESCO report, an *annual* financing gap of 39 billion USD will have to be met from 2015–2030, totaling 585 billion USD over the fifteen-year period, if the international community is to achieve universal pre-primary, primary, and secondary education of decent quality in low and lower-middle income countries.

Delivering the right to education has far-reaching benefits. The Global Partnership for Education estimates that the increase in women's education, for instance, has prevented over four million child deaths. Similarly, if all children were to acquire basic reading skills, the Partnership estimates that 171 million people would be lifted from poverty, a reduction in global poverty rates of 12 percent. Over 40 years, a mere 0.1 percent improvement in a country's educational equality can increase per capita GDP by 23 percent.

e. Summary

In our examination of the implementation of select rights in the Declaration – which looked beyond the representative rights we have listed here – a number of themes emerged.

First, the UDHR represents the founding document in a process of progressive elaboration of human rights. As we approach the 70th anniversary of the Declaration, this achievement should be celebrated.

Second, historic progress has been made in the promotion and protection of rights since 1948, including the development of a body of human rights law and implementation mechanisms that simply could not have been envisioned in the 1920s and 1930s. It is vital to account for, understand, and take this development seriously as a platform for further progress.

Third, despite the gains, we must recognize and respond to the reality that human rights continue to be violated on an alarming scale across the globe, even by nations that have signed the relevant human rights treaties. Our case studies demonstrate that it is the poorest people and countries, and the most vulnerable members of society – particularly women and children, ethnic and religious minorities, migrants and refugees, and persons with disabilities – who are most susceptible to human rights violations. They also remind us that violations are conducted and perpetuated not only by states, but also by international organizations, corporations, and private persons.

Fourth, the fullness of human rights will only be achieved through multiple overlapping and coordinated mechanisms. We need mechanisms that operate at both the international and national levels, and which engage both governmental and non-governmental institutions. Human rights education also has an indispensable role to play.

The Commission hopes that the brief case studies appended illustrate the great challenges that remain in achieving the widespread and regular application and enforcement of human rights standards. It is beyond the scope of the Commission's work to examine the full range of mechanisms that promote and protect rights. Instead we have identified four areas for particular analysis: first, the UN system of human rights implementation; second, national and regional legal systems; third, non-governmental organizations; and fourth, human rights education. In singling out these four areas, the Commission does not suggest that other mechanisms are not important. They are. The project of human rights implementation will require ongoing analysis, review, and hard work in the decades ahead.

6.3 Suggestions on implementation

a. Recommendations for strengthening the UN system on human rights implementation

Much action is still needed to ensure that the rights so eloquently espoused in the UDHR, and codified by the later covenants and conventions, are made realities in life as well as law. In this section, the Commission supports a number of existing proposals for improving the UN system for the protection of human rights. We call on the UN to establish a commission to consider these and other proposals for realizing Article 28 of the Declaration.

i. Implement the recommendations of UN human rights mechanisms

There are different human rights monitoring mechanisms in the United Nations system, based either on the UN Charter or on UN treaties. The most prominent Charter-based bodies are the Human Rights Council and its regime of Special Procedures and the Universal Periodic Review (**UPR**). Of the ten current human rights treaty bodies, nine monitor implementation of the core international human rights treaties while the Subcommittee on Prevention of Torture monitors places of detention in states that are party to the Optional Protocol to the Convention against Torture.

The UN human rights mechanisms produce a rich array of findings, decisions, and recommendations, many on a country-by-country basis, including recommendations adopted by treaty bodies after examining the implementation of a human rights treaty by a state party; recommendations issued by Special Procedures of the Human Rights Council in reports on country visits, thematic reports, and communications on individual cases; recommendations stemming from the UPR; and recommendations of commissions of inquiry, fact-finding missions, and other *ad hoc* human rights investigations initiated by the Human Rights Council, the Security Council, the High Commissioner for Human Rights, or the UN Secretary-General.

But the problems and priorities identified through UN human rights mechanisms do not command sufficient attention and action from the international community and the UN as a whole, including its security and development endeavors. The UN should enhance its system-wide support and follow-up aimed at ensuring the findings, decisions, and recommendations made – country by country – by the UN's human rights mechanisms are enforced through a better alignment between human rights and development. For instance, the OECD Development Assistance Committee should recognize that, in order to be effective, official development assistance must increasingly address the good governance, rule of law, and human rights gaps revealed by the human rights mechanisms, especially when recipient countries accept and agree with stipulated changes.

ii. Enhance the OHCHR's field presence

Away from its headquarters in Geneva, the operations of the Office of the High Commissioner for Human Rights' (**OHCHR**) can be strategic entry points for pursuing human rights at country level, integrating a human rights perspective into the work of United Nations country teams and peace missions, and strengthening national institutions and civil society. OHCHR's field operations already scrutinize the human rights situations in specific countries, while also building the capacity of Member States and other duty-bearers to address shortfalls and abuses.

Over the years, the OHCHR has gradually widened its presence in the field; however, its operations are not yet fully fit for purpose. First, OHCHR is underrepresented: it has 65 field presences but only 13 country offices – compared to the World Bank or United Nations Development Programme, for example, which maintain permanent offices in well over 100 member countries. Moreover, the OHCHR's regional offices provide no coverage in North-East Asia, South Asia, and North America. Second, its field operations are underfunded. Indeed human rights account for less than 3 percent of the UN's regular budget, which inhibits the ability of the OHCHR to effectively monitor and champion human rights on the ground.

The UN should expand the OHCHR's regional and country field presence and significantly raise its financial support for priority human rights activities in line with countries' legal obligations and political commitments made in the UPR. This is crucial to strengthening national human rights protection systems through development cooperation as well as peace-keeping and peace-building budgets. It will enhance the prevention of violations and the success and sustainability of peace and development efforts.

Of course, none of this is of any consequence unless states cooperate with, allow access for, and do not inhibit or intimidate UN personnel seeking to promote and protect rights and to investigate alleged abuses.

iii. Raise human rights concerns for consideration by the UN Security Council

There is no formal procedure permitting UN human rights bodies to take the initiative in raising an issue for consideration by the Security Council. In recent years, it has become increasingly common for the OHCHR and the Special Procedures of the Human Rights Council to brief the Security Council through an informal procedure known as the "Arria-formula." However, such sessions can be convened only at the initiative of a member or members of the Security Council and then the extent to which such sessions are convened depends on the Presidency of the Council.

Human rights concerns are root causes of conflict, and early action by the UN system and the international community can prove critical in averting violence. The Secretary-General already has the power under Article 99 of the UN Charter to bring to the Security Council any matter that may threaten the maintenance of international peace and security. We urge the Secretary-General to exercise this power whenever advised to do so by the High Commissioner for Human Rights, the Special Procedures of the Human Rights Council, or the heads of the human rights components of UN peace missions.

iv. Limit the UN Security Council veto in the case of mass atrocities

Again and again, vetoes or threats of vetoes by permanent members (*the P5*) have blocked Security Council action to maintain international peace and security in a range of crises. The Council's inability to act on behalf of civilians in Syria and elsewhere has not only had a massive cost in human life, but has dangerously eroded the credibility of the UN system. Inaction has given the green light to perpetrators to engage in ever more flagrant human rights abuses.

To address this, France has proposed that the P5 voluntarily suspend veto rights in situations involving mass atrocities. In the wake of the events in Syria, France has argued that such a step would enhance the legitimacy of the Security Council, strengthen its integrity, restore the power of discussion and constructive negotiation, and convey the will of the international community to make the protection of human life a true priority. The logic here is clear: when the misuse of the veto blocks action to stem atrocities, it contravenes the principles of the UN. All Member States should support the French initiative for restraining the veto in the case of mass atrocities.

More generally, the P5 should accept an affirmative obligation to offer a reasoned justification for *any* exercise of the veto, and to propose an alternative plan in accordance with international law to achieve the same objectives.

v. Harness technology to enhance human rights accountability

Advances in technology since 1948, and particularly the creation of the Internet, present an unprecedented opportunity to amplify human rights accountability. The UN should encourage and enable the development at the country level – by national human rights institutions and (currently only a few) Parliaments' Human Rights Committees – of online platforms through which citizens can rate their governments' performance on human rights issues. This can empower citizens to exert pressure on governments responsible for violations.

In addition, we recommend a direct mechanism supported by the UN, which could take two forms. First, an online "complaint clearinghouse" would let citizens register complaints about human rights abuses directly with the UN. The clearinghouse would help overcome existing data shortcomings on human rights and enable the OHCHR and other human rights mechanisms to target their activities more accurately. Second, a global human rights wiki, accessible to and editable by recognized human rights organizations, would equip the relevant actors to readily combine and share data regarding ongoing crises, improving both the speed and effectiveness of global responses. The UN should consider these measures and others to harness new forms of technology that can widen the writ and reach of human rights for all in the twenty-first century.

As such mechanisms are put in place, we should meet the inevitable need to provide protection and security for those who take the risk of identifying and complaining about human rights violations. Encryption of the relevant technology can have the effect of encouraging people to submit testimony and evidence that might then be put to good use by the international community.

b. National and regional legal systems

Many of the suggestions we have made have to do with global institutions and NGOs. However, we should never forget a point we have stressed a number of times in this document, that the front-line work of upholding human rights is always conducted under the auspices of national constitutions and bills of rights. They are intended to provide primary protections, through national legal systems. And any account of implementation must look to them, in the first instance, because at too many times and in too many places, between the intention and the reality falls a dark shadow.

This implies that, as we scrutinize the human rights records of particular countries, we should pay attention not only to their constitutional arrangements, but also to the work that is being done by lawyers and rights-related NGOs in those countries. So, for example, no account of human rights implementation in the United States can be complete without a full account of the way in which state and national bills of rights operate, nor without an account of the way in which bar associations and groups like the American Civil Liberties

Union advocate for the protection of rights domestically. The point is perhaps obvious in the case of the United States. It may be less obvious in developing nations and emerging democracies, where there is a temptation to think that all the work has to be done by outside agencies assisting with development and nation-building.

The judiciary has a pivotal role to play in upholding human rights. Only an independent judiciary can render justice impartially on the basis of law, thereby assuring the rights and fundamental freedoms of the individual. The basic principle is laid down in Article 10 of the UDHR: "everyone is entitled in full equality to a fair and public hearing by an independent and impartial tribunal, in the determination of his rights and obligations and of any criminal charge against him." In this era, however, in country after country, there has been a rising wave of attacks on the independence of judges, lawyers, prosecutors, and court officials, particularly in the form of threats, intimidation, and interference in the discharge of their professional functions. The international community must redouble its resolve to safeguard and enhance the independence and effectiveness of judiciaries worldwide, in line with existing international principles of the rule of law.

Consistent with this imperative, the international community should pay attention to the impact of statutes of limitation governing human rights claims. California became the first American jurisdiction, through recently enacted legislation, to offer survivors of abuse a longer period of time to bring their claims to court. This legislation – California Assembly Bill 15 – extended the period from two years to 10 years for serious transgressions such as torture, war crimes, extrajudicial killing, crimes against humanity, and human trafficking. This reform should provoke a wide-ranging discussion of the procedural obstacles to the effective implementation of human rights.

Regional human rights courts are and can be powerful instruments for the vindication of human rights. This is the purpose of the European Court of Human Rights, the Inter-American Court of Human Rights, and the African Court on Human and Peoples' Rights. The international community should aim to bolster the role of these institutions, ensuring that they have both sufficient resources and competent personnel. The international community should also encourage the development of new regional human rights courts by the League of Arab States and in Asia and the Pacific. These courts should hear complaints not only from state parties, but also from individuals. All UN Member States should agree to submit themselves to the authority of international tribunals whose jurisdiction can appropriately – geographically or otherwise – be extended to them. Given that compliance has not always been automatic, we reiterate that state parties have a binding obligation under the treaties creating these courts to give effect to their rulings.

At the global level, the UN should consider the creation of a World Human Rights Court, consistent with the principle of complementarity. While this is presently an aspiration, considered and considerable thought should be given to whether a World Human Rights Court could reinforce the maintenance of human rights across the globe.

c. NGOs

The implementation of human rights does not depend just on official institutions. It presupposes and is enriched by a vigilant civil society at national, regional, and international levels. The Human Rights Council already accredits a number of NGOs specifically dedicated to human rights. Such organizations play a frontline role in highlighting the importance of the rights protected in the UDHR, in drawing attention to shortcomings in their implementation, and in naming and shaming governments that are guilty of violations or of failing to protect their citizens from human rights abuses. In light of this, it is especially important that states make reasonable accommodation for NGOs aiming to promote, protect, and investigate violations of human rights.

d. Human rights education

i. The UDHR and human rights education for all

The preamble of the UDHR states that "every individual and every organ of society shall strive by teaching and education to promote respect for these rights and freedoms."

ii. The UDHR and human rights education since 1948

Since 1948, the ideals of the UDHR and later instruments have gained greater acceptance and achieved greater realization, and human rights education (**HRE**) has advanced alongside this. In the first few decades after the UDHR, HRE consisted mostly of legal training focused on the formal standards codified by the UN and other intergovernmental organizations, or else popular education carried out by NGOs in the global south. In the 1970s, UNESCO promoted HRE, and social movements adopted human rights discourse to support legal campaigns for the effectuation of human rights at the national and international levels. Meanwhile, as national educational systems were expanding in scope and competence across the world, newer and older democracies alike started and continued to incorporate HRE into formal education, although mostly in the legal rather than the popular sphere.

UNESCO's third congress on HRE in Montreal in 1993 proposed a world plan of action on education for human rights and democracy, endorsed that same year by the World Conference on Human Rights in Vienna, which proposed a Decade for Human Rights Education. The next year, with the support of HRE NGOs, the UN General Assembly proclaimed that decade would run from 1995 to 2004. The General Assembly created a World Programme for HRE in 2005, and in 2012 adopted the United Nations Declaration on Human Rights Education and Training, which outlined the obligations of states and other duty-bearers to implement HRE universally. It mandated educational training, information, awareness-raising, and learning activities aimed at promoting universal respect for and observance of all human rights and fundamental freedoms. The aim was to prevent violations and abuses by providing people with knowledge, skills, and understanding to shape their own attitudes and behaviors – thus empowering them as active agents in the building and strengthening of a universal culture of human rights.

The leading international network of HRE actors is HRE2020: The Global Coalition for Human Rights Education. This alliance was formed by NGOs in 2014 to encourage and enhance the HRE compliance of states by raising awareness and urging progress, by integrating HRE into UN mechanisms, and by monitoring the implementation of HRE commitments. The coalition has set the year 2020 as a benchmark for assessing the performance of governments, international institutions, and civil society in providing access to quality human rights education.

iii. Transformative human rights education

HRE is necessarily diverse in goals, content, and delivery. Some educational reforms that followed from the UN's Decade for Human Rights Education involved little more than incorporating human rights language into the educational standards or textbooks of Member States. The integration of HRE into formal school curricula can be the most effective way to broadly execute HRE; but a simultaneous community-based approach to HRE can help ensure that school children educated in HRE do not encounter resistance outside the classroom door.

"Transformative HRE" is a community-based approach to HRE, intended for children, youth, and adults in formal or non-formal settings, and including cognitive, affective, and action-oriented elements. Contextualized and relevant studies are paired with interactive learning to bring human rights to life and to foster in students and citizens an awareness of global citizenship and a respect for human rights. Transformative HRE exposes gaps between rights and realities, and provokes group dialogue on the specific steps essential to closing the gaps. Learners engage in critical reflection, open discussion, and individual and collective action to move the cause of human rights forward locally, nationally, and globally. Transformative HRE can yield remarkable results for individuals and groups.

iv. Advancing transformative human rights education

Fostering a universal culture of human rights among all individuals and institutions through transformative HRE "from the bottom up" can add important impetus to the adoption and enforcement of legal standards by governments "from the top down."

Yet many states lack a national HRE plan for formal education; many with a plan do not implement it well; and many who implement HRE focus on its basic legal literacy rather than advancing its transformative potential. NGOs and other civil society organizations have been the most active promoters and implementers of HRE, campaigning for the incorporation of HRE into formal education. The Commission calls on all governments, international organizations, and NGOs to encourage and support transformative human rights education.

We see our work as part of a process of public education about human rights, not as an ending, but as a beginning that must be carried forward. Further details of ongoing HRE initiatives are found in Online Appendix D.[3]

6.4 Sovereignty

In addition to the suggestions in the previous section, we must also consider deeper structural issues that make the implementation of human rights more or less successful. The most prominent is the issue of national sovereignty. Although, as we stressed in section 6.3(b), much implementation can be achieved within the legal system of particular countries, the pressure for progress must sometimes come from the outside. If domestic policy fails or if human rights are systemically flouted within a particular society, external pressure may have to come to the assistance of those whose rights are threatened.

Accordingly, no account of implementation can dispense with the general issue of sovereignty and the way in which it has come to be viewed in the new era of global human rights consciousness.

a. General (human rights as limits on sovereignty)

The era of human rights that was initiated by the UDHR has certainly disposed of any notion of state sovereignty that purports to insulate states from external criticism of internal rights violations. Occasionally we hear countries invoke that insular and outdated notion of sovereignty, but such claims are increasingly half-hearted and no longer treated as

---

3   Appendix D, on Human Rights Education, is available at https://www.openbook publishers.com/isbn/9781783742189#resources. This Appendix was prepared for the Commission by a working group on human rights education under the auspices of the Center on Global Justice (University of California, San Diego).

credible by the international community. Countries change in their willingness to accept and listen to criticism from beyond their borders. In any case, such criticism – including public official comment – is not to be equated with intervention. Nor is it to be rebutted with the rationalization that violations are internal matters and "none of the outside state's business." One principle the UDHR represents, and rightly so, is that human rights in every country are the world's business. To that extent, the rights culture inculcated by the UDHR has to a real degree transformed the world of sovereign states.

The intermediate case is where nations or members of the international community sponsor NGOs or perhaps opposition parties within another state – sponsorship that can be characterized as an attempt to influence the political process of the target state. This is a question on which there is considerable disagreement. It is not a matter on which the UDHR takes sides, except perhaps implicitly in the proclamation clause's insistence that "every organ of society [...] shall strive [...] to promote respect for these rights."

We should not regard it as a failure of the UDHR that it does not resolve questions like this. They are worked out more effectively in the terms of the Covenants. But the Commission wishes to affirm: first, that countries may not misuse their national sovereignty as an excuse for insulating themselves from external pressure on human rights; and second, that it is legitimate for states to raise human rights issues in conducting foreign relations.

b. Sanctions, denunciations, and other measures

The international community needs a toolkit of governmental and multilateral responses to rights violations that is more legitimate and more sophisticated than we have today, and which relies on mechanisms other than the use of force. There are many instruments of change used: some widely acknowledged, like trade sanctions; some far less recognized, such as human rights "name and shame" mechanisms; and others perhaps less clearly articulated, such as providing shelter to migrants fleeing from neighboring countries in times of great distress. Armed force is seldom the best option. We recommend that a study be undertaken of what governments do when they genuinely want to seek to change another government's behavior, and what governments are susceptible to in terms of real world pressures on human rights.

c. Responsibility to Protect

The Responsibility to Protect – known as RtoP – refers to the obligation of states toward their populations and toward all populations at risk of genocide and other mass atrocities.

Though the international community – as part of the doctrine of RtoP – has reserved the right to intervene militarily in countries where grave and widespread violations are underway, that has been and is likely to remain an exceptional occurrence. We can say that in such cases, human rights do represent a limit on state sovereignty. But since the most flagrant cases will be rare, and since individual rights violations on a smaller scale will remain quite frequent, there are questions about state sovereignty and human rights that have to be resolved in the case of less dramatic violations. Thus, in our view it is wrong to ignore the wider challenge and rivet attention exclusively on RtoP and the instances where it may be invoked.

RtoP stipulates three pillars of responsibility: first, every state has the Responsibility to Protect its people from four grave crimes – genocide, war crimes, crimes against humanity, and ethnic cleansing; second, the wider international community has the responsibility to encourage and assist individual states in meeting that obligation; and third, if a state is manifestly failing to protect its people, the international community must be prepared to take appropriate collective action in a timely and decisive manner and in accordance with the UN Charter.

These principles originated in a 2001 report of the International Commission on Intervention and State Sovereignty and were endorsed by the United Nations General Assembly in the 2005 World Summit Outcome Document. In January of 2009, the UN Secretary-General released a report on implementing the Responsibility to Protect, followed in July by the first General Assembly debate on the issue. During the debate, UN Member States overwhelmingly reaffirmed the 2005 commitment and the General Assembly passed a consensus resolution (A/RES/63/308) taking note of the Secretary-General's report.

Since then, the Responsibility to Protect has featured prominently in a number of resolutions adopted by the Security Council, including those in relation to Libya (2011), Côte d'Ivoire (2011), Yemen (2011), Mali (2012), Syria (2014), South Sudan (2014), and the Central African Republic (2015).

The Commission supports the concept of RtoP governing the process of humanitarian intervention. However, intervention under the auspices of RtoP will be far from regular and will be appropriate only in the case of egregious and widespread human rights violations. Such intervention is certainly justified. But it is no substitute for routine responsibility for the rights of individuals and it cannot be the main focus of our analysis of responsibility for rights. Instead we should look, wherever possible, to the regular institutional arrangements in each society, not just to a few dramatic cases.

We have to emphasize that in the final analysis rights are an individual matter. Every person has rights. And the violation of rights, the erosion of rights, or the failure to fulfill rights are matters of concern, even when they are not widespread. For example, when a particular woman or man is tortured or detained without trial, there may be no prospect of any international military mobilization: but a human right has been trampled on. Too much concentration on RtoP can lead us to assume that human rights violations only become serious when they are *en masse* and egregious. In a general sense, out of our common humanity, we all have a responsibility with regard to any violation – even if it is only sporadic or individual.

The specter of mass atrocity must never lead us to overlook the wrong that is done when any human right is violated at a lesser level. Any time a violation occurs – which may affect one person or one thousand – we must take notice. Underpinning this imperative is the principle that the violation of the rights of anyone is the concern of everyone. Of course, in the first instance it is the province of every national legal system to deal with human rights violations within that country. The international human rights community becomes involved either when this national responsibility falters, or when the rights violations reach a certain level of frequency or severity. We know that there is a challenge of setting priorities here. Not all of us can be on duty all the time. But nobody is entitled to say of any human rights violation that it is, in principle, "none of my business."

When an international response is appropriate, it should be chosen from a range of options, depending on circumstances. The selected response should be consistent with the protection of other rights. It should be proportionate to the violation; you cannot deploy armed force over an issue of educational reform. The question must be: "Is this response producing a net gain for human rights or not?" For the danger is not just failing to act, but doing more harm than good. On the range of possible actions, military intervention for the Rwanda genocide would be at the far end; but the range also spans diplomatic démarches, sanctions, formal findings by state departments, informal protests, and raising issues at a ministerial level. One of the advantages of this approach is that the need for coordination mounts at the far end of the range, but does not necessarily accrue at the near end. If there is any question of armed intervention, that is an issue for the Security Council. If there is a question of sanctions, that is a matter for the international community. If denunciation is the right option, it is not clear that we need Security Council clearance. And countries have unilaterally taken up the task of naming and shaming rights violators. Therefore, we should confine a requirement for some authoritative multilateral declaration to the far end of the spectrum: military intervention, and perhaps sanctions too.

7. Human Rights and a Global Ethic

The promulgation of the UDHR in 1948 made a difference in how people saw their place in the world and their relations with their state and with each other. This is in itself a valuable contribution, quite apart from the securing of the rights actually listed in the document. Over the decades since 1948, the UDHR has provided the rudiments of a "common conscience" for humanity. To borrow the words of Immanuel Kant, a violation of rights in any place is now felt all around the world. The international community is continuing to build on this, and the UDHR should be regarded as one of the pillars of a modern global ethic.

Understandings of a "global ethic" will vary. But the idea seems to comprise at least the following two elements: first, a set of fundamental ethical ideas (such as human dignity) that are globally accepted as establishing a basis on which people deal with one another in the world; and second, a set of principles that arise out of the development of a new kind of interdependent global civil society, with common opportunities and common dangers. The Commission believes that a globalizing world needs an ethic of global citizenship, even if we cannot agree on a moral universalist basis for it.

Of course, although human rights are important for a global ethic, they are only a part of it. Other pillars of a global ethic include:

- Good governance and the rule of law, at both national and global levels.

- Responsibility for planet and climate, and our obligations to future generations.

           http://dx.doi.org/10.11647/OBP.0091.12

- Basic humanitarian responsibility for one another, even when human rights are not directly involved.

- The eradication of extreme poverty.

- Outlawing aggressive war and upholding international security through the United Nations system as a basis for the resolution of global conflict.

- The elimination of nuclear weapons and other weapons of mass destruction.

- A broad commitment to strengthening institutions such as the United Nations and its agencies, which have paramount responsibility for the well-being of the international system.

- The maintenance of the cosmopolitan frameworks that enable people to relate to one another scientifically, productively, economically, and culturally all around the world.

These pillars are related to one another and they form an integrated system. Each of them has pivotal human rights dimensions but each of them also takes us beyond the field of human rights and opens up broader vistas of global obligation and participation. One way of thinking about human rights requirements is that they secure the foundation on which people can exercise and construct their citizenship responsibilities, whether in their own countries or in the world at large. Without the protections and liberty that human rights are supposed to secure, it would be difficult for people to lift their gaze beyond their immediate fears and deprivations.

We think it is imperative, therefore, to reaffirm that human rights in general and the UDHR in particular contribute immensely to the emergence of a global ethic. A global ethic is not the same as international law. It is something like the shared moral impulse that underlies and sustains international law. Many things need to be comprised in a global ethic cannot be laid down in precise legal terms. At the same time, the reality of human rights institutions and the evolution of international human rights law – along with national and regional declarations of rights, and their accompanying courts – demonstrate that it is possible to build real-world institutions and practices upon these ethical foundations.

The stated foundations of the UDHR – particularly the principles of dignity and human solidarity and the rejection of the barbarism that was experienced in the middle of the twentieth century – are the centerpiece of an emerging global ethic. The UDHR illustrates this not just by stating foundational values in its preamble but by showing how various human rights flow from these deeper commitments. In this regard, the very idea of rights is key. The distinctiveness of the contribution made by human rights to the global ethic is that they represent the responsibilities that are owed to every individual man, woman, and child on the planet. While some rights are group rights, in the final analysis the idea of human rights conveys a commitment to the liberty and well-being of individuals. It represents a commitment to the principle that no person, however lowly, is to be sacrificed simply for the well-being of others.

The adoption of the UDHR also demonstrates the prospects and challenges for ethical consensus in a diverse world. We acknowledge that, in a sense, its formulations are quite abstract in relation to the rich global array of cultures, ethics, and religions. But the fact of its adoption and its longevity indicate that it is possible to identify common commitments and common respect for humanity.

As part of a global ethic, the UDHR has great educational force and great importance in building and sustaining morale among people who are vulnerable to various forms of oppression. It provides a common point of reference for them and a conviction that they are not alone in resisting abuses. The Declaration legitimizes their struggles.

Equally, the Universal Declaration of Human Rights and its progeny have been indispensable in de-legitimizing human rights abuses. The conviction is now abroad in the world that violating human rights is something that no person, state, or entity is entitled to do and for which they may properly be held accountable by the world community at every level.

Appendix A:
The Universal Declaration of Human Rights

*Note: the below text has been annotated with labels for each of the clauses and provisions (**in bold**). The Commission refers to these labels throughout the report.*

PREAMBLE

a) **[the inherent dignity clause]** Whereas recognition of the inherent dignity and of the equal and inalienable rights of all members of the human family is the foundation of freedom, justice and peace in the world,

b) **[the barbarism and aspiration clause]** Whereas disregard and contempt for human rights have resulted in barbarous acts which have outraged the conscience of mankind, and the advent of a world in which human beings shall enjoy freedom of speech and belief and freedom from fear and want has been proclaimed as the highest aspiration of the common people,

c) **[the rebellion clause]** Whereas it is essential, if man is not to be compelled to have recourse, as a last resort, to rebellion against tyranny and oppression, that human rights should be protected by the rule of law,

d) **[the friendly relations clause]** Whereas it is essential to promote the development of friendly relations between nations,

e) **[the United Nations clause]** Whereas the peoples of the United Nations have in the Charter reaffirmed their faith in fundamental human rights, in the dignity and worth of the human person and in the equal rights of men and women and have determined to promote social progress and better standards of life in larger freedom,

f) **[the pledge of respect clause]** Whereas Member States have pledged themselves to achieve, in co-operation with the United Nations, the promotion of universal respect for and observance of human rights and fundamental freedoms,

g) **[the common understanding clause]** Whereas a common understanding of these rights and freedoms is of the greatest importance for the full realization of this pledge,

h) **[the proclamation clause]** Now, Therefore THE GENERAL ASSEMBLY proclaims THIS UNIVERSAL DECLARATION OF HUMAN RIGHTS as a common standard of achievement for all peoples and all nations, to the end that every individual and every organ of society, keeping this Declaration constantly in mind, shall strive by teaching and education to promote respect for these rights and freedoms and by progressive measures, national and international, to secure their universal and effective recognition and observance, both among the peoples of Member States themselves and among the peoples of territories under their jurisdiction.

Article 1. **[the free and equal provision]** All human beings are born free and equal in dignity and rights. They are endowed with reason and conscience and should act towards one another in a spirit of brotherhood.

Article 2. **[the universality provision]** Everyone is entitled to all the rights and freedoms set forth in this Declaration, without distinction of any kind, such as race, colour, sex, language, religion, political or other opinion, national or social origin, property, birth or other status. Furthermore, no distinction shall be made on the basis of the political, jurisdictional or international status of the country or territory to which a person belongs, whether it be independent, trust, non-self-governing or under any other limitation of sovereignty.

Article 3. **[the right to life provision]** Everyone has the right to life, liberty and security of person.

Article 4. **[the anti-slavery provision]** No one shall be held in slavery or servitude; slavery and the slave trade shall be prohibited in all their forms.

Article 5. **[the anti-torture provision]** No one shall be subjected to torture or to cruel, inhuman or degrading treatment or punishment.

Article 6. **[the legal personality provision]** Everyone has the right to recognition everywhere as a person before the law.

Article 7. **[the non-discrimination provision]** All are equal before the law and are entitled without any discrimination to equal protection of the law. All are entitled to equal protection against any discrimination in violation of this Declaration and against any incitement to such discrimination.

Article 8. **[the remedies provision]** Everyone has the right to an effective remedy by the competent national tribunals for acts violating the fundamental rights granted him by the constitution or by law.

Article 9. **[the arbitrary arrest provision]** No one shall be subjected to arbitrary arrest, detention or exile.

Article 10. **[the right to a hearing provision]** Everyone is entitled in full equality to a fair and public hearing by an independent and impartial tribunal, in the determination of his rights and obligations and of any criminal charge against him.

Article 11. **[the due process provision]** (1) Everyone charged with a penal offence has the right to be presumed innocent until proved guilty according to law in a public trial at which he has had all the guarantees necessary for his defence. (2) No one shall be held guilty of any penal offence on account of any act or omission which did not constitute a penal offence, under national or international law, at the time when it was committed. Nor shall a heavier penalty be imposed than the one that was applicable at the time the penal offence was committed.

Article 12. **[the privacy and reputation provision]** No one shall be subjected to arbitrary interference with his privacy, family, home or correspondence, nor to attacks upon his honour and reputation. Everyone has the right to the protection of the law against such interference or attacks.

Article 13. **[the freedom of movement provision]** (1) Everyone has the right to freedom of movement and residence within the borders of each state. (2) Everyone has the right to leave any country, including his own, and to return to his country.

Article 14. **[the asylum provision]** (1) Everyone has the right to seek and to enjoy in other countries asylum from persecution. (2) This right may not be invoked in the case of prosecutions genuinely arising from non-political crimes or from acts contrary to the purposes and principles of the United Nations.

Article 15. **[the nationality provision]** (1) Everyone has the right to a nationality. (2) No one shall be arbitrarily deprived of his nationality nor denied the right to change his nationality.

Article 16. **[the marriage and family provision]** (1) Men and women of full age, without any limitation due to race, nationality or religion, have the right to marry and to found a family. They are entitled to equal rights as to marriage, during marriage and at its dissolution. (2) Marriage shall be entered into only with the free and full consent of the intending spouses. (3) The family is the natural and fundamental group unit of society and is entitled to protection by society and the State.

Article 17. **[the property provision]** (1) Everyone has the right to own property alone as well as in association with others. (2) No one shall be arbitrarily deprived of his property.

Article 18. **[the thought and worship provision]** Everyone has the right to freedom of thought, conscience and religion; this right includes freedom to change his religion or belief, and freedom, either alone or in community with others and in public or private, to manifest his religion or belief in teaching, practice, worship and observance.

Article 19. **[the free expression provision]** Everyone has the right to freedom of opinion and expression; this right includes freedom to hold opinions without interference and to seek, receive and impart information and ideas through any media and regardless of frontiers.

Article 20. **[the free association provision]** (1) Everyone has the right to freedom of peaceful assembly and association. (2) No one may be compelled to belong to an association.

Article 21. **[the democracy provision]** (1) Everyone has the right to take part in the government of his country, directly or through freely chosen representatives. (2) Everyone has the right of equal access to public service in his country. (3) The will of the people shall be the basis of the authority of government; this will shall be expressed in periodic and genuine elections which shall be by universal and equal suffrage and shall be held by secret vote or by equivalent free voting procedures.

Article 22. **[the general social security provision]** Everyone, as a member of society, has the right to social security and is entitled to realization, through national effort and international co-operation and in accordance with the organization and resources of each State, of the economic, social and cultural rights indispensable for his dignity and the free development of his personality.

Article 23. **[the conditions of work provision]** (1) Everyone has the right to work, to free choice of employment, to just and favourable conditions of work and to protection against unemployment. (2) Everyone, without any discrimination, has the right to equal pay for equal work. (3) Everyone who works has the right to just and favourable remuneration ensuring for himself and his family an existence worthy of human dignity, and supplemented, if necessary, by other means of social protection. (4) Everyone has the right to form and to join trade unions for the protection of his interests.

Article 24. **[the rest and leisure provision]** Everyone has the right to rest and leisure, including reasonable limitation of working hours and periodic holidays with pay.

Article 25. **[the standard of living provision]** (1) Everyone has the right to a standard of living adequate for the health and well-being of himself and of his family, including food, clothing, housing and medical care and necessary social services, and the right to security in the event of unemployment, sickness, disability, widowhood, old age or other lack of livelihood in circumstances beyond his control. (2) Motherhood and childhood are entitled to special care and assistance. All children, whether born in or out of wedlock, shall enjoy the same social protection.

Article 26. **[the education provision]** (1) Everyone has the right to education. Education shall be free, at least in the elementary and fundamental stages. Elementary education shall be compulsory. Technical and professional education shall be made generally available and higher education shall be equally accessible to all on the basis of merit. (2) Education shall be directed to the full development of the human personality and to the strengthening of respect for human rights and fundamental freedoms. It shall promote understanding, tolerance and friendship among all nations, racial or religious groups, and shall further the activities of the United Nations for the maintenance of peace. (3) Parents have a prior right to choose the kind of education that shall be given to their children.

Article 27. **[the cultural life provision]** (1) Everyone has the right freely to participate in the cultural life of the community, to enjoy the arts and to share in scientific advancement and its benefits. (2) Everyone has the right to the protection of the moral and material interests resulting from any scientific, literary or artistic production of which he is the author.

Article 28. **[the international order provision]** Everyone is entitled to a social and international order in which the rights and freedoms set forth in this Declaration can be fully realized.

Article 29. **[the duties and limitation provision]** (1) Everyone has duties to the community in which alone the free and full development of his personality is possible. (2) In the exercise of his rights and freedoms, everyone shall be subject only to such limitations as are determined by law solely for the purpose of securing due recognition and respect for the rights and freedoms of others and of meeting the just requirements of morality, public order and the general welfare in a democratic society.

(3) These rights and freedoms may in no case be exercised contrary to the purposes and principles of the United Nations.

Article 30. **[the no-abuse provision]** Nothing in this Declaration may be interpreted as implying for any State, group or person any right to engage in any activity or to perform any act aimed at the destruction of any of the rights and freedoms set forth herein.

Appendix B:
Members of the Commission

K. Anthony Appiah

Kwame Anthony Appiah is Professor of Philosophy and Law at New York University. He was born in London, grew up in Ghana, and studied philosophy at Cambridge University. He has taught philosophy in Ghana, France, Britain, and the United States. Among his books are *In My Father's House: Africa in the Philosophy of Culture* (1992) and *Cosmopolitanism: Ethics in a World of Strangers* (2006). Professor Appiah has been President of the PEN American Center and of the Modern Language Association and Chair of the Board of the American Philosophical Association and the American Council of Learned Societies.

Laurel Bellows

Laurel Bellows, founding principal of the Bellows Law Group, P.C. is past president of the American Bar Association, the Chicago Bar Association, and International Women's Forum Chicago. Laurel is currently serving on the Executive Committee of the InterAmerican Bar Association. She is an internationally recognized business lawyer. Her law firm offers strategic business counseling and litigation to businesses of all sizes, counseling senior executives and corporations on executive employment, severance agreements, workplace disputes, anti-trafficking risk assessment, supply chain and recruiting policies, and cybersecurity. Laurel is licensed to practice in Illinois, Florida, and California. She is an arbitrator and certified mediator.

Nicolas Berggruen

Nicolas Berggruen is Chairman of the Berggruen Institute. The Institute develops and implements systemic political governance projects and thinking. Through its Philosophy and Culture Center, it fosters fresh ideas and understanding between the East and the West. Committed to leaving a legacy of art and architecture, he sits on the boards of the Museum Berggruen, Berlin and the Los Angeles County Museum of Art. He has worked with some of the world's leading architects on projects from India to Turkey and the USA.

Paul Boghossian

Paul Boghossian is Julius Silver Professor of Philosophy at New York University and Director of its Global Institute for Advanced Study. Elected to the American Academy of Arts and Sciences in 2012, he has written on a wide range of topics including knowledge, meaning, rules, moral relativism, aesthetics, and the concept of genocide. He is the author of *Fear of Knowledge: Against Relativism and Constructivism* (2006) and *Content and Justification: Philosophical Papers* (2008); and editor, with Christopher Peacocke, of *New Essays on the A Priori* (2000). A volume collecting a series of his exchanges with Timothy Williamson on the topics of *a priori* and analytic truth is forthcoming from Oxford University Press.

Gordon Brown

Gordon Brown served as Prime Minister of the United Kingdom from 2007 to 2010, Chancellor of the Exchequer from 1997 to 2007, and as a Member of Parliament in his home county of Fife, Scotland, from 1983 to 2015. He is the United Nations Special Envoy for Global Education and a passionate advocate for the rights of children. He believes every girl and boy deserves the opportunity of a future through schooling. Mr. Brown has also been appointed Chair of the new Global Commission on Financing Global Education and serves as New York University's inaugural Distinguished Global Leader in Residence.

Craig Calhoun

Craig Calhoun is Director of the London School of Economics and calls it "the dream job for anyone who cares about social science, global issues, and bringing better knowledge to public debates." In the USA, he was President of the Social Science Research Council, and taught at the University of North Carolina, Columbia, and NYU, where he was most recently University Professor of Social Sciences and Director of the Institute for Public Knowledge.

Calhoun's many publications bring together theory and empirical research across several disciplines. Among his books on politics and social movements are *Neither Gods Nor Emperors: Students and the Struggle for Democracy in China* (1994) and *The Roots of Radicalism* (2012). He has also published extensively on nationalism and globalization; secularism, religion, and the public sphere; economic and technological change; critical social theory; and the history of social science.

Wang Chenguang

Wang Chenguang holds a B.A. (1980), Master of Law (1983), and Ph.D. in Law (1999) from Peking University, as well as an LL.M. (1986) from Harvard Law School. He has taught as Teaching Assistant (1983), Lecturer (1985), and Associate Professor (1991) at Peking University; as University Senior Lecturer (1994) at City University of Hong Kong; and as Associate Professor (2000) and Professor (2000) at Tsinghua University. He has served as Dean (2002–2008) at Tsinghua University Law School, and he is currently Vice-Chair of the China Association of Legal Theory, Deputy-Chair of the China Association of Legal Education, Deputy-Chair of the China Association of Health Law, Executive Chief-Editor of the *China Journal of Legal Science* (English), and Legal Advisor to the China Food and Drug Administration. His fields of teaching and research are legal theory, comparative law, health law, legal clinic, legislative and judicial systems.

Mohamed ElBaradei

Mohamed ElBaradei was Director General of the International Atomic Energy Agency (IAEA) and is currently Director General Emeritus. He was born in Egypt and holds degrees in Law from the University of Cairo and the New York University School of Law. He was an Egyptian diplomat before joining the IAEA in 1984. In 2005, he was jointly awarded with the IAEA the Nobel Peace Prize. He has received numerous other awards and *Honoris Causae* for his work as a public servant and advocate of tolerance, humanity, and freedom. He played a leading role in the Arab Spring of 2011.

Fonna Forman

Fonna Forman is a professor of Political Theory and Founding Director of the Center on Global Justice at the University of California, San Diego. She is best known for her revisionist scholarship on Adam Smith, recuperating the ethical, social, spatial, and public dimensions of his thought. Her current work focuses on human rights at the urban scale, climate justice in cities, and equitable urban development in the Global South. She presently serves as Vice-Chair of the University of California Climate Solutions Group. She is a principal in Estudio Teddy Cruz + Forman, a research-based political and architectural practice based in San Diego/ Tijuana.

Andrew Forrest

Andrew Forrest is a leading philanthropist and businessman who joined the Giving Pledge campaign, contributing wealth generated from founding two of Australia's major resource companies and employers.

Internationally, the five global initiatives of Andrew's Walk Free Foundation are helping to bring an end to modern slavery. The Foundation facilitated the historical signing of a declaration by the major world faiths to reject slavery and publishes the Global Slavery Index: achievements without precedent. At home, Andrew works to end the disparity between indigenous and non-indigenous Australians through GenerationOne's education, training, and employment efforts. His businesses have allocated $2bn to indigenous contractors, and recently he chaired the Prime Minister and Cabinet's national Indigenous Review, "Creating Parity."

Ronald M. George

Ronald M. George is a 1961 graduate of Princeton University's Woodrow Wilson School of Public and International Affairs, and a 1964 graduate of Stanford Law School. From 1965 to 1972, he served as a Deputy Attorney General in the California Department of Justice, where he represented the State of California in six oral arguments before the United States Supreme Court. He was appointed to the Los Angeles Municipal Court by Governor Reagan, to the Superior Court by Governor Brown, Jr., to the Court of Appeal by Governor Deukmejian, to the California Supreme Court by Governor Wilson as an Associate Justice, and, in 1996, as the 27th Chief Justice of California (confirmed in 1998 by the voters for a 12-year term.) As Chief Justice he chaired the Judicial Council of California and the Commission on Judicial Appointments. He was inducted as a Fellow of the American Academy of Arts and Sciences in 2009 and served as President of the Conference of Chief Justices, Chair of the Board of Directors of the National Center for State Courts, and as a member of the steering committee of the Sandra Day O'Connor Project on the State of the Judiciary.

Asma Jahangir

Twice Chairperson of the Human Rights Commission of Pakistan, Asma Jahangir was elected President of the Supreme Court Bar Association of Pakistan in 2011. Asma is also a Director of the AGHS Legal Aid Cell, which provides free legal assistance to the needy and was instrumental in the formation of the Punjab Women Lawyers Association in 1980 and the Women Action Forum in 1985.

In 1998, Asma was appointed United Nations Special Rapporteur on Extrajudicial, Summary or Arbitrary Execution as part of the Commission on Human Rights, and in 2004 she was appointed United Nations Special Rapporteur on Freedom of Religion or Belief for the Council of Human Rights.

John Agyekum Kufuor

John Kufuor is the Former President of Ghana (2001–2009). He was called to the Bar, Lincoln's Inn, London (1959–1961); BA Honours (PPE) and MA Economics, Oxford (1964).

In December 2013, he was appointed UN Secretary-General's Special Envoy on Climate Change. In 2012, he founded the John A Kufuor Foundation for Leadership, Governance, and Development. In 2011, he was named joint-winner of the World Food Prize with former Brazilian President Lula da Silva. As Ghanaian president, he was Chairperson of the African Union (2007–2008) and Chairman of the Economic Community of West African States (2003–2005).

Other appointments held include Co-Chairman of the Global Panel on Agriculture and Food Systems for Nutrition (2013); Chairman of the Governing Council, Interpeace (2010–2015); Global Envoy for the Neglected Tropical Diseases Alliance (2011–2015); Chairman of the Sanitation and Water for All Partnership (2011–2015); Deputy Minister of Foreign Affairs (1969–1972); and Member of Parliament (1969–1972 and 1979–1981).

Graça Machel

Graça Machel is a renowned international advocate for women's and children's rights and has been a social and political activist over many decades. She is a former freedom fighter and was the first Education Minister of Mozambique. Her contributions to the Africa Progress Panel, the United Nations Secretary-General's Millennium Development Goals Advocacy Group and the High-Level Panel on Post 2015 Development Agenda, have been widely appreciated. She is a member of The Elders, Girls Not Brides, Board Chair of the Partnership for Maternal, Newborn & Child Health, African Ambassador for A Promised Renewed, President of SOAS, University of London, Chancellor of the University of Cape Town, Board Chair of the African Centre for the Constructive

Resolution of Disputes, President of the Foundation for Community Development, and founder of the Zizile Institute for Child Development.

As Founder of the newly established Graça Machel Trust, she has focused more recently on advocating for women's economic and financial empowerment, education for all, an end to child marriage, food security and nutrition, and promoting democracy and good governance.

Catherine O'Regan

Kate O'Regan served as a judge of the Constitutional Court of South Africa from 1994–2009 and has been serving as an *ad hoc* judge of the Supreme Court of Namibia since 2010. From 2008–2012, she served as the inaugural chairperson of the United Nations Internal Justice Council, a body established to ensure independence, professionalism, and accountability in the internal system of justice in the UN. She is Visiting Professor in the Faculty of Law at the University of Oxford and also serves on the boards of many NGOs working in the fields of democracy, the rule of law, human rights, and equality.

Ricken Patel

Ricken Patel is the founding President and Executive Director of Avaaz.org, a global civic movement for social change which has rapidly grown since 2007 into the largest online activist community in the world, with over 40 million members in all 193 countries represented at the United Nations. Ricken was voted "Ultimate Gamechanger in Politics" by the Huffington Post and named a Young Global Leader by the Davos World Economic Forum. He was also among *Foreign Policy*'s 100 Top Global Thinkers in 2012. He has lived and worked in Sierra Leone, Liberia, Afghanistan, and Sudan, working on conflict resolution for various organizations including the International Crisis Group and the

International Center for Transitional Justice. Ricken holds a Master's degree in Public Policy from the Kennedy School of Government at Harvard University, and a Bachelor's in Philosophy, Politics and Economics from Balliol College, Oxford University.

Emma Rothschild

Emma Rothschild is Director of the Joint Center for History and Economics, and Jeremy and Jane Knowles Professor of History at Harvard University. She is a Fellow of Magdalene College, Cambridge. She was Chairman of the United Nations Research Fund for Social Development from 1999–2005 and a member of the United Nations Foundation Board from 1998–2015. She has written extensively on economic history and the history of economic thought. Her publications include *The Inner Life of Empires: An Eighteenth-Century History* (2011) and *Economic Sentiments: Adam Smith, Condorcet and the Enlightenment* (2001).

Robert E. Rubin

Robert Rubin served as the 70th Secretary of the U.S. Treasury from 1995 to 1999. He joined the Clinton Administration in 1993 as the first director of the National Economic Council.

Mr. Rubin began his career in finance at Goldman Sachs, rising to Vice-Chairman and Co-Chief Operating Officer (1987–1990) and Co-Senior Partner and Co-Chairman (1990–1992). He was a member of the board at Citigroup and a senior advisor to the company (1999–2009). In 2010, he joined Centerview Partners as a senior counselor.

Mr. Rubin is Co-Chairman of the Council on Foreign Relations; is on the Board of the Mount Sinai Health System; and is Chairman of the Board of the Local Initiatives Support Corporation.

Jonathan Sacks

A global religious leader, philosopher, bestselling author, and moral voice for our time, Rabbi Lord Jonathan Sacks was recently named the winner of the 2016 Templeton Prize. Rabbi Sacks is currently the Ingeborg and Ira Rennert Global Distinguished Professor of Judaic Thought at New York University and the Kressel and Ephrat Family University Professor of Jewish Thought at Yeshiva University. He is Emeritus Professor of Law, Ethics and the Bible at King's College London. Previously, Rabbi Sacks served as Chief Rabbi of the United Hebrew Congregations of the Commonwealth between September 1991 and September 2013, only the sixth incumbent since the role was formalized in 1845.

Kailash Satyarthi

Mr Satyarthi has been a tireless advocate of children's rights for over three decades. He and the grassroots movement founded by him, Bachpan Bachao Andolan (Save the Childhood Movement), have liberated more than 84,000 children from exploitation and developed a successful model for their education and rehabilitation. Mr Satyarthi has been the architect of the single largest civil society network for the most exploited children, the Global March Against Child Labour, whose mobilization of unions, civil society and most importantly, children, led to the adoption of ILO Convention 182 on the worst forms of child labour in 1999. He is also the founding president of the Global Campaign for Education, an exemplar civil society movement working to end the global education crisis, and GoodWeave International which raises consumer awareness in the carpet industry. In 2014, he was jointly awarded the Nobel Peace Prize for "struggle against the suppression of children and young people and for the right of all children to education."

Klaus Schwab

Klaus Schwab is the founder and Executive Chairman of the World Economic Forum, the International Organization for Public-Private Cooperation, based in Geneva, Switzerland. Schwab studied at the Swiss Federal Institute of Technology in Zurich, at the University of Fribourg, and at Harvard University. His degrees include doctorates in Mechanical Engineering and Economics (*summa cum laude*). From 1972–2003, he was Professor of Business Policy, University of Geneva. In 1998, Schwab co-founded, with his wife Hilde, the Schwab Foundation for Social Entrepreneurship, supporting social innovation around the world; in 2004, he founded the Forum of Young Global Leaders; and in 2011, he founded the Global Shapers Community. He has received numerous honorary doctorates and honorary professorships, as well as the highest international and national honors for initiatives undertaken in the spirit of entrepreneurship in the global public interest and for peace and reconciliation.

Amartya Sen

Amartya Sen is Thomas W. Lamont University Professor and Professor of Economics and Philosophy at Harvard University. Until 2004 he was Master of Trinity College, Cambridge. He has served as President of the American Economic Association, the Indian Economic Association, the International Economic Association, and the Econometric Society. His awards include Bharat Ratna (India); Commandeur de la Légion d'Honneur (France); the National Humanities Medal (USA); Honorary Companion of Honour (UK); Ordem do Merito Cientifico (Brazil); the Aztec Eagle (Mexico), and the Nobel Prize in Economics. Sen's books, on economics, philosophy, decision theory, and social inequalities have been translated into more than thirty languages.

John Sexton

John Sexton served as President of New York University from 2002 through 2015. He is NYU's Benjamin Butler Professor of Law and Dean Emeritus of the Law School. Milestones of his tenure include the growth of NYU's global network, encompassing campuses in Abu Dhabi and Shanghai; a merger with Polytechnic University, now the NYU Tandon School of Engineering; and the largest increase in the Arts and Science Faculty in the University's history.

A Fellow of the American Academy of Arts and Sciences, President Emeritus Sexton also serves on the board of the Institute of International Education and is past Chair of the American Council on Education. Photo Credit ©NYU Photo Bureau: Gallo

Robert M. Shrum

Robert M. Shrum holds the Carmen H. and Louis Warschaw Chair in Practical Politics and is Professor of the Practice of Political Science at the University of Southern California. For decades, he was a political strategist and consultant, serving as senior advisor to Kerry 2004 and Gore 2000 campaigns. He was also senior advisor to the campaign of Prime Minister Ehud Barak of Israel and to the British Labour Party. Mr. Shrum has written for *New York Magazine*, *The Los Angeles Times*, *The New York Times*, and *Newsweek*, among other publications. His book, *No Excuses: Concessions of a Serial Campaigner* (2007), was a national bestseller.

Jeremy Waldron

Jeremy Waldron is University Professor and Professor of Law at New York University. Professor Waldron was educated in New Zealand and at Oxford, and his career has included appointments at Edinburgh, Berkeley, Columbia, and Oxford. He is well-known for his work on constitutionalism, human dignity, historic injustice, national security issues, and the rule of law. His books include *Law and Disagreement* (1999) and *Torture, Terror and Trade-offs: Philosophy for the White House* (2010). His new book *Political Theory* is being published by Harvard University Press in March 2016. Professor Waldron was elected to the American Academy of Arts and Sciences in 1998 and has been a Fellow of the British Academy since 2011.

Joseph Weiler

J.H.H. Weiler is President of the European University Institute (EUI), and University Professor at NYU Law School. Previously he served as Manley Hudson Professor of International Law at Harvard Law School and subsequently as Director of the Jean Monnet Center at NYU School of Law. He also served for many years as Member of the Committee of Jurists of the Institutional Affairs Committee of the European Parliament. Prof. Weiler is Editor-in-Chief of the *European Journal of International Law* (EJIL) and the *International Journal of Constitutional Law* (ICON). He is also an Honorary Professor at University College London and the University of Copenhagen, and Co-Director of the Academy of International Trade Law in Macao, China. He holds a PhD in European Law from the EUI, Florence and honorary degrees from various European and American universities. He is the author of several books and articles in the field of European integration, international and comparative constitutional law, and human rights law.

Rowan Williams

Rowan Williams took up the mastership of Magdalene College, Cambridge on January 1, 2013. He took his degrees at Christ's College, Cambridge and at Christ Church and Wadham College, Oxford. His career began as a lecturer at Mirfield (1975–1977), and he later returned to Cambridge as Tutor and Director of Studies at Westcott House. After ordination in Ely Cathedral, and serving as Honorary Assistant Priest at St George's Chesterton, he was appointed to a University Lectureship in Divinity. In 1984, he was elected a Fellow and Dean of Clare College. Then, still only 36, it was back to Oxford as Lady Margaret Professor of Divinity for six years, before becoming Bishop of Monmouth and, from 2000, Archbishop of Wales. In 2002, Dr. Williams was confirmed as the 104th Archbishop of Canterbury.

Diane C. Yu

Diane C. Yu is serving as Counselor to Leadership and Executive Director of the Sheikh Mohamed bin Zayed Community Programs at New York University Abu Dhabi, one of the three New York University campuses. From 2012-2015 she was NYU's Deputy President, a member of the President's cabinet, and presidential advisor regarding dealings with NYU Trustees, deans, faculty, administrators, and students; prior to that she served for 10 years as the Chief of Staff and Deputy to the NYU President. Before coming to NYU, she was Managing Counsel at a Fortune 250 company, General Counsel for the State Bar of California (for whom she won a case in the U.S. Supreme Court), White House Fellow, and California Superior Court Commissioner. She has a B.A. from Oberlin College and a J.D. from U.C. Berkeley.

Appendix C:
Members of the Philosophers' Committee

Philip Alston	New York University Law School
Anthony Appiah	New York University Law School and Department of Philosophy
Charles Beitz	Princeton University, Department of Politics
Seyla Benhabib	Yale University, Departments of Political Science and Philosophy
Simon Caney	Oxford University, Department of Politics and International Relations
Fonna Forman	University of California, San Diego, Department of Political Science
Avishai Margalit	Hebrew University of Jerusalem, Department of Philosophy
Pratap Mehta	Center for Policy Research, New Delhi
Samuel Moyn	Harvard University Law School and Department of History
Onora O'Neill	Cambridge University, Department of Philosophy
Michael Rosen	Harvard University, Department of Government
Michael Sandel	Harvard University, Department of Government
Amartya Sen	Harvard University, Department of Economics
John Tasioulas	King's College London Law School
Jeremy Waldron	New York University Law School
Wang Chenguang	Tsinghua University Law School
Joseph Weiler	European University Institute

This book need not end here...

At Open Book Publishers, we are changing the nature of the traditional academic book. The title you have just read will not be left on a library shelf, but will be accessed online by hundreds of readers each month across the globe. OBP publishes only the best academic work: each title passes through a rigorous peer-review process. We make all our books free to read online so that students, researchers and members of the public who can't afford a printed edition will have access to the same ideas.

This book and additional content is available at:
http://www.openbookpublishers.com/isbn/9781783742189

Customize

Personalize your copy of this book or design new books using OBP and third-party material. Take chapters or whole books from our published list and make a special edition, a new anthology or an illuminating coursepack. Each customized edition will be produced as a paperback and a downloadable PDF. Find out more at:

http://www.openbookpublishers.com/section/59/1

Donate

If you enjoyed this book, and feel that research like this should be available to all readers, regardless of their income, please think about donating to us. We do not operate for profit and all donations, as with all other revenue we generate, will be used to finance new Open Access publications.

http://www.openbookpublishers.com/section/13/1/support-us

Like Open Book Publishers

Follow @OpenBookPublish

Read more at the Open Book Publishers BLOG

You may also be interested in:

Democracy and Power
The Delhi Lectures
Noam Chomsky. Introduction by Jean Drèze

https://www.openbookpublishers.com/product/300

Peace and Democratic Society
Edited by Amartya Sen

http://www.openbookpublishers.com/product/78

Tolerance
The Beacon of the Enlightenment
Translated by Caroline Warman, et al.

http://www.openbookpublishers.com/product/418

Lightning Source UK Ltd.
Milton Keynes UK
UKOW06f1251130516

274185UK00004B/17/P